DPH Management Series

Supervisory Management

J M DEWAN • K N SUDARSHAN

DISCOVERY PUBLISHING HOUSE
NEW DELHI-110002

First Published - 1996

Reprinted - 2014

ISBN: 978-81-7141-353-9

Supervisory Management

Published by:

DISCOVERY PUBLISHING HOUSE PVT. LTD.
4383/4B, Ansari Road, Darya Ganj
New Delhi-110 002 (India)
Phone: +91-11-23279245, 43596064-65
Fax: +91-11-23253475
E-mail: discoverypublishinghouse@gmail.com
sales@discoverypublishinggroup.com
web: www.discoverypublishinggroup.com

Printed at:
Infinity Imaging Systems
Delhi

Preface

The management world is in transition. The causes of this transition are many, but the major one is the vast changes in knowledge and in the information that flows in and out of organizations. This changing information disrupts traditions, established processes, well-known procedures, and routine ways of doing things. New principles, concepts, techniques, ideas, expressions, processes, and procedures are emerging, moving us to a new plateau of professional practice. Trying to capture this changing knowledge and information is like trying to capture the atmosphere. How can you do it when the atmosphere is continually shifting and when you need the atmosphere to do the capturing? The best we can do is find a peak from which we can at least get a perspective on management as a whole, decide on the work and responsibilities of management, and gather in whatever practical management information we can. A team of experts in this series represent some of the best contemporary thinking and information available. They represent many major successful corporations, active consulting agencies, and well-known educational institutions, and all are experts on what is happening with the flow of knowledge and information in the management world. This is a lofty pinnacle from which to survey the management world.

Managers and supervisors clamor for current information and guidelines to help solve formidable problems in their work world—problems that range from "how to do it" to "how to resolve conflict when doing it." Many problems are generated from miscommunication and incompetence. As the management practice proceeds from the complex to the supercomplex, problem solving becomes a large-scale challenge requiring new knowledge and skills. Managers and supervisors cannot wait for research breakthroughs with real-world answers to solve these dilemmas. They must tackle them here and now with the useful information and proven practices immediately available. Whether making a decision, solving a problem setting up a procedure, designing a process, or resolving a behaviour conflict, a manager must rely heavily on information. To a great extent, management practitioners are information workers; that is, they generate, distribute, store, retrieve, and consume information. Competence in finding and using the right information at the needed time determines to a considerable extent competence in the management function, activity, or responsibility. The *DPH Management Series* attempts to fill this need for usable information in spite of the changing nature of its subject.

The *DPH Management Series* not a book to be read and later discarded. It is a reference book, a tool to be used by managerial personnel in the day-to-day work of an organization. Like a tool, it should never be more than a reach away when a new situation emerges that demands its use. This series aim to achieve a first-and practical and proven knowledge and information as a self-development opportunity for those who are moving into or upward in management. A complete spectrum of management subjects is immediately available for orientation, study, analysis, assimilation, and problem solving. Within one set of covers is the view of management as a totality. The management field is loaded with ideas that the organization of this handbook series unique logic. It follows both levels and areas of responsibilities of an organization.

The work of this handbook series is the collaborative effort of many outstanding people in the management field. The motivation for this work varied from individual to individual, but the central motivation that united us all was the excitement of capturing the management state-of-the-art and sharing it with colleagues in the dynamic profession of management.

This series should be of great help to managerial practitioners at any organizational level who are responsible for a function, department, or set of responsibilities. The handbook series will also give these practitioners insights into management roles and approaches in other areas as well. The subject matter encompasses top, middle, and lower management. Special emphasis was placed on managing people, time, space, budgets, and resources to give the handbook extra utility for middle and lower management. Students of management in university or educational institutions will find the series an invaluable resource for adding "real world" practices to their academic and theoretical foundations. MBA students will gain an invaluable overview of the total organization to complement their MBA degree. Administrators and public managers can become acquainted with practices employed by managers and supervisors in private organizations. These practices are not always directly applicable in public sector bodies, but with thought and modifications, these private practices can adapt to public organizations. Public and university librarians will find the handbook an indispensable reference for the multitude of questions on many topics from the general public, special groups, associations, and students.

Editors

Contents

1 The Supervisor and Supervisory Role

Introduction

Competent supervisor are essential in any business. However many supervisors are poorly trained, neglected by management, usually blamed for unproductive employees and resented by trade union representatives.

Unfortunately many managers do not fully understand the supervisor's role, consequently weak support creates poor relations between supervisors, employees and trade unions. Indeed UK managers fall below standards set in other developed countries. This fault increases the burden on supervisors who must adapt to difficult situations, aggravated now by the accelerating challenge of implementing information technology and other technologies in the workplace.

Effects of the computer

More powerful computer networks have given senior management the opportunity to remove whole layers of middle management. Many specialists, such as accountants and stock controllers, have faced redundancy as much of their work can be done more cheaply and accurately by machine. Senior management has therefore been brought closer to workers. With the aid of networks, more individuals can manage and control themselves. The computer-literate people remaining after lay offs emerge with new roles, new career patterns and more mobility.

Clearly this continual restructuring process creates opportunities for well-trained supervisors as more computer-illiterate individuals retire or become redundant and networking improves. Supervisory development programmes should therefore be a part of top management's strategy.

Definitions of the role of supervisor

This involves looking at the role from traditional and modern viewpoints, taking into account current trends. All tend to conflict. There are four common organisational supervisory categories:

- Supervisors
- managers
- supervision
- management.

In later chapters these terms are discussed in detail and related to organisational and operating problems.

The traditional view

From this viewpoint, a supervisor is any person who is given authority and responsibility for planing and controlling the work of a group through close contact.

In the broad sense, this definition means that

supervisors may be delegated the authority to deal with the following matters:

- engagement, transfer, reprimand and dismissal of staff under their control
- staff grievances
- staff discipline
- quantity and quality of output
- recommendations to management.

In the narrow sense it can include anyone who directs the work of others by:

- giving instructions on operations
- co-ordinating specialist departments
- recommending courses of action to management.

This classical approach is commonplace, fits the traditional, formal organisation's method of operation and conforms to may organisation principles described in the next chapter.

The modern view

This is based upon acceptance of supervisors as a part of management and as managers, but the *term* supervisor remains. Typical definitions from this viewpoint are:

- the supervisor is the key front-line manager, the person who can make or break top management plan.
- the supervisor is any manager who control non-managerial subordinates and is wholly accountable for their work

- supervisors, managers and any others who are responsible for the work of people, at any level and in any type of organisation, should regard themselves as managers.

Current trends

These are emerging as a result of the increasing impact of information technology and the realisation that individual initiatives are essential if productivity is to be improved. Such trends give rise to the following:

- the development of direct relationship between supervisors and senior managers through computerised systems, which implies that the concept of an organisational hierarchy is now at least partially redundant
- supervisors adopting a collaborative approach, coaching employees who are established in autonomous teams; such coaching - in collaborative management terms - means close control is removed and replaced with a rapport where team members ask for advice and feel free to discuss their weaknesses and strengths.

Distinguishing features of a supervisor

Five main role relationships remain, regardless of these variations in defining the role of supervisor. These distinguish more clearly the differences between a supervisor and a manager in organisational thinking.

Technician level

Usually a three-tier organisational structure may be identified:

1 higher technology
2 technology
3 technician levels.

In the first tier a specialist controls the technological specialists; in the second tier these specialists control a range of technicians; and in the third tier technicians control the operators and clerical staff.

Sector membership

Supervisory sector membership extends to all organisational levels as all managers and supervisors have a group they are responsible for. The distinguishing feature for supervisors is non-membership of the management sector, which is clearly differentiated by differences in salary, working conditions, status and perks. Although the latter feature conflicts with modern definitions, in practice a demarcation line is apparent to everyone.

Restricted policy interpretation

simplified, top management makes policy, middle management broadly interprets policy, while lower management is restricted to narrow interpretations, which ensure that the day-to-day running of sections conforms.

Decision making

Senior managers make strategic decisions that have a broad effect, such as on marketing, products and services, growth finance, organisation structure, public relations and personnel. Middle managers make tactical decisions to implement the strategies through the use of resources, allocation of duties and various means of control.

Works supervisors make operational decisions involving, say, synchronising production, stock control, labour and machine utilisation and adjustments to the production schedule, while office supervisors make similar decisions on administrative aspects.

Workload limitation

Critical variables affecting the load or stress on a supervisory or managerial job determine the appropriate level and grading. Typical features are the degree of similarity to jobs performed by subordinates, complexity of planning and control, proximity of subordinates to each other, complexity of tasks performed and the degree of supervision imposed by maturity and training levels of subordinates. Theoretically as complexity of features increases, the education, training, qualifications and experience should increase, determining the category and suitability of the individual for that category. Unfortunately this may not always occur in practice, mainly because selection procedures are faulty.

Summary of similarities and differences

To clarify the definitions discussed and avoid blurring later, the similarities between supervisors and managers are outline first, followed by the main differences.

Similarities

These are as follows:

- they are responsible for the work of other people
- they use similar principles, practices and techniques and develop an art to achieve results
- some roles coincide, typically leader, liaison work, various communication activities, handling disturbances and negotiator
- they conform to loose definitions of management, such as the art of dealing with people, the art of getting things done through people and to forecast, plan, organise, command, co-ordinate and control.

Differences

These are as follows:

- additional managerial roles are mainly figure head, entrepreneur, resource allocator and giver of technological expertise
- managers are involved in long-term direction and control of employees as well as short-term activities
- managers conform to comprehensive definitions emphasising policy, strategy, entrepreneurial activities, overall direction and control and technological and specialisms expertise
- managers make strategic and tactical decisions

at senior and middle management levels respectively, while supervisors make operational decisions.

Range of supervisor jobs

No two supervisory jobs are exactly alike. Two apparently similar supervisory jobs may in be very different, depending on such factors as status, company size, the product, the type of company and its structure, relationships between management, supervision, trade unions and operators, production tempo, growth problems, staffing and the use of specialists.

This variation in supervisory jobs depends mainly upon the range of duties, the complexity of each duty and the particular level of supervision. an understanding of the latter aspect is most important.

The many levels of supervision can be grouped in a number of ways, depending on such factors as titles, salary, number of employees controlled, degree of authority and responsibility. Grouping based on the last two factors, for example, can be further divided into four sub-groups: primary group supervision, section supervision, department supervision and works and administration supervision. These are discussed below. In most cases a supervisor will fit into one of these groups. Generally all four levels are seen in medium and large size companies whereas in the small firm only the second and last would operate.

Primary group supervision

Included are chief clerks, leading hands and charge-hands who are responsible for supervising small groups. This cluster forms a primary working group headed by a primary group leader.

Section supervision

This level generally includes about six primary group leaders headed by a section supervisor, junior foreman, assistant foreman or office supervisor.

A section supervisor rarely does any manual work; instead authority and responsibility is generally restricted to allocating duties, ensuring smooth work flow by co-ordinating the activities of the primary group leaders and dealing with the day-to-day running of the section.

Department supervision

A control group of about six sections is headed by a foreman, department supervisor or department superintendent. General responsibility for the department includes planning and controlling the work.

Works and administration supervision

All senior supervisors come under this category. There are many titles used, including general foreman, senior foreman, production foreman, shop supervisor, shop superintendent and office manager. Whatever the title, the job carries substantial authority and responsibility for effectively controlling the six to eight departments that generally make up the shop, works or office.

Supervisors and employees

In general terms, the difference between employees and their supervisors is that employees perform their own work using their technical knowledge manually, whereas supervisors control the work of others using their technical knowledge theoretically combined with supervisory techniques.

In modern terms the supervisor should concentrate more on developing the co-operation and direct involvement of employees who, it is hoped, will behave more responsibly and feel committed as result. emphasis is placed on teamwork, participation, autonomy and flexibility - key factors that allow employees to work within much wider control limits. Indeed, the supervisor must adopt roles associated strongly with co-ordination, advice, adaptability and associated specialisms, to be successful.

Often logical changes are not acceptable to employees through fear of the consequences, such as less autonomy or redundancy. This apprehension may be reduced by discussion in advance, divulging plans, noting responses and suggestions and endeavouring to gain support. Without ample discussion the supervisor risks ridicule. The usual accusations are discourtesy, ignorance, lack of understanding and having no idea of employees' capabilities and experience.

The old saying still hold good: treat adults like children and they will behave like them; treat them like dogs and they may bite; treat them like idiots and they will behave like them.

Basic elements of supervision

The three basic elements, which are the titles of the three parts of this book, each contain many aspects that demand appropriate techniques, some of which are used instinctively by applying sound common sense. Others demand training and practice. applying the right principles at the right time needs something more than knowledge alone as the basic elements must interact closely, although they are outlined independently.

A representative sample of ten supervisory activities is given for each basic element in. These activities or duties are interdependent in practice.

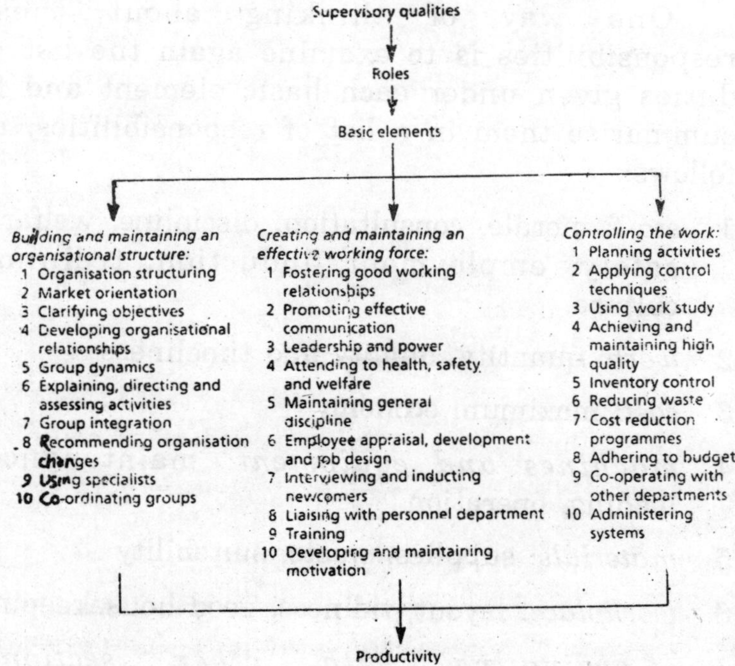

Fig. The basic elements of supervision

For instance no decision should be made on facts and theory alone; the human factor must be given due consideration, along with control features in a given situation. Finding and maintaining the right balance is difficult, time-consuming and often frustrating.

Responsibilities of a supervisor

A supervisor is responsible for subordinates, the activities and the workplace that he or she is given formal authority to control. Within this overall definition, the finer points of responsibility should now emerge that make possible the performance of the job.

One way of thinking about these responsibilities is to examine again the list of duties given under each basic element and to summarise them in a list of responsibilities, as follows:

1 *staff*: morale, consultation, discipline, welfare, safety, employment, induction, training, culture.

2 *work*: quantity, quality and timeliness

3 *cost*: maximum economy

4 *machines and equipment*: maintenance, loading, operation

5 *materials*: supplies, waste, suitability

6 *workplace*: layout, tidiness, good housekeeping

7 *co-ordinating with other sections*: organisational culture.

The above responsibilities can only be fulfilled by giving the supervisor the authority to forecast and plan in accordance with company policy, to organise and execute, to co-ordinate and control. The supervisor, in turn, becomes responsible for these activities.

Social responsibilities

The wider field of social responsibilities covers indirect relationship with the shareholders, the customers, the state and the suppliers. Although these social groups appear remote from supervision, their interests must be considered if a supervisor is to realise his or her full responsibility.

The shareholders or proprietors have invested capital in the business and, naturally, they expect it to earn interest in the form of dividend. The customers expect goods to be priced in relation to quality and delivered on time. Unfortunately, the latter point is often considered too lightly, bearing in mind the chaos late delivery can cause, especially with goods for industry. The question of better designs and a wider range of products for the community presents deeper problems of research, cost and profitability.

The state relies upon industry and everyone connected with it to provide sufficient goods to export and to supply the home market. Economic stability is vital to everyone; success depends largely upon the best use of capital and the effectiveness of labour.

Finally, the supervisor's responsibility to suppliers or customers means that promises should be kept whenever possible and wrong impressions carefully avoided. For example, the impression that regular supplies of a commodity will be needed is easily created, leading a supplier to plan accordingly, whereas a limited quantity only may be actually required. Any information of use to the supplier should be given freely, especially on the question of specifications which may be unnecessarily fine, such as tolerances, finish and packing.

Quality of a good supervisor

The main problem when discussing personal qualities is the measurement of degree. For example, when people refer to intelligence as a quality, they use such terms as average, reasonable, high level, low level and average level. Unfortunately there is no standardised method of dealing with these matters and each individual will naturally interpret these terms in a slightly different way.

It should be appreciated that a general foreman may possess no more qualities than a primary group leader, but he or she will possess them in greater degree. Moreover, a comprehensive list of an outstanding general foreman's qualities would correspond with specifications for general management. Nevertheless, the same qualities appear at the lower levels of supervision, but in a less intensive form.

The main differences in supervisory job specifications occur in the technical and administrative aspects, which vary considerably depending upon the industry, company size of different circumstances within the same factory, e.g., special qualities may be desirable in supervising particular groups that contain an unusual feature.

The five essential qualities are:

drive

leadership

intelligence

skills and knowledge

character

They are discussed below, but not in order of importance as each job demand a different proportion of all these requirements.

Drive

The basic need for vitality, energy and enthusiasm is good health. Physical and mental fatigue impair judgement and are demoralising for subordinates who need to be enthused by the supervisor's example and vigour. Making the best use of time and energy requires careful planning. Whenever possible, over-excitement and bursts of stop-gap measures should be avoided to conserve nervous energy. An even spread of effort sustained over long periods is desirable for good performance, which can then be expected from others. This sustained effort or drive demands self-discipline and conscientiousness in the face of outside distractions and the general pace of living.

Leadership

A good leadership must be an outstanding member of the group who gets along easily with people and has above-average competence. Leadership is difficult to define accurately; its intangible qualities cannot be learned, yet they are easily recognisable.

Naturally, ability is not enough. Previous environment, which moulds personality and character, should provide a balanced background for an individual to feel at ease, mix easily with many types of people and sense the ability to supervise well. some people, of course, manage to overcome an unhappy past, while others who were more fortunate fail to make the grade.

Good leaders set high standard of performance for themselves, keep to them and expect similar performance from others. They mix easily with people by understanding them and using clear and constructive methods of handling everyday problems. They are not always more skillful or more intelligent than their subordinates, but they appreciate their own technical and human limitations. They recognise their responsibilities and use their authority in a fair and impartial manner. This implies that they are temperamentally suited for the task of solving problems, are sufficiently far sighted to see potential ones before they arise and can take appropriate early action.

An important management task is to create conditions under which leaders can become effective but, at the same time, avoiding the development of a situation where leaders struggle for power among each other. If the well-known rat race is allowed, subordinates suffer and organisation is badly affected. Given the opportunity and the right conditions, the leader can push people beyond their normal capabilities towards a higher level of effectiveness, with greater work satisfaction.

Intelligence

Most supervisory posts require intelligence, similar to the general level of intelligence found among skilled operators. Some people expect supervisors to be more intelligent than their subordinates, which is naturally desirable.

A high level of intelligence is essential in some supervisory jobs, where technical and administrative problems are intricate and demanding. On the other hand, many supervisory jobs contain a large proportion of routine work that would soon frustrate the highly intelligent person.

In reality, supervisors need shrewdness, judgement and an acute mind with plenty of common sense. They must be quick-witted, able to distinguish between major and minor problems, apportioning sufficient time to deal with each problem. They must decide whether permanent or temporary arrangements are needed. They must understand clearly the many and varied written and spoken instructions and be able to pass on information clearly to a number of different types of subordinates.

Skills and knowledge

Three main skills are distinguishable: technical, interpersonal and conceptual. They apply to all managerial and supervisory jobs but the ratios between them differ, depending on the organisational level.

As top levels are approached, technical skills tend to reduce, interpersonal skills should remain the same, while conceptual skills increase. Understandably collaborative philosophies demand more emphasis on interpersonal and conceptual skills for supervisors as a crucial appreciation of the total organisation and the involvement of employees are needed to achieve high performance levels.

These two skills are majority supervisory assets, rated above many other qualities such as IQ, knowledge and job skills.

Technical skills

An inherent part of any supervisory job is technical competence. Supervisors need a good knowledge of every operation or process under their control to be able to eliminate common faults, wastage and any dangerous practices. Practical and theoretical knowledge plus varied experience help to command respect and help others.

To train successfully, supervisors should illustrate:

- *why* a job should be done, so that the criteria used are seen to be right for that task
- *how* it should be done, to demonstrate the proper use of all the knowledge available
- to be aware always that the trainee may be able to contribute through his or her own knowledge or ideas and be innovative.

At the same time a questioning approach should be adopted to discover any problems the trainees may have. Supervisors do not necessarily have to be the best operator in the group, but certainly they should not be the worst.

A reasonable elementary education and further education are essential. Technical skills are learned relatively quickly by repetition and are specific to particular activities. They are classified by referring to an established management principle or methodology and are measurable. Implementation and appraisal are learned through practice. A general definition is the capability to apply knowledge, experience, techniques and methods, to perform specific tasks with the aid of appropriate machines and equipment.

Interpersonal skills

Often called human skills or interactive skills, they use motivational and behaviourist techniques to extract higher performance. They stimulate ideas, concentrate on needs and goals and encourage participation.

A general definition is the capability and judgement to work with employees and to utilise fully their talents through leadership and various behavioural theories. Generally they take a long time to develop as learning and experience are needed, along with patience, perseverance and tolerance.

Sound interpersonal relationships are viewed occasionally as difficult to achieve because of cultural and subcultural factors. These vary widely between countries, areas within countries and with company size. Although some variations in managerial behaviour patterns are noticeable between countries, organisational structuring mostly follows logical patterns that dominate managerial behaviour patterns. On a broader basis interpersonal skills are also applied between management and suppliers, customers, the community, and the government.

Conceptual skills

Abstract in nature, these multiple skills are drawn from knowledge and experience over a long period. for further development the opportunity to gain insight into corporate activities and problems is essential.

Conceptual skills concentrate on broader issues, corporate and organisational planning and policy and systems. Collectively, a definition is the capability to act in accordance with the objectives of the company as a whole. Unfortunately conflict often exists between the objectives visualised by the group or section and those of the corporate whole.

The development of though processes that improve conceptual skills requires specialised training, perseverance and close examination of experiences. The mental process of attempting to visualise the future includes not only using data available and experiences, but, also, utilising many aids such as check-lists, systems procedures, statistical frameworks and models. Such forecasting does not rely upon trends or data, but more upon intuition to identify important relevant features and mentally classifying events into significant areas that have causal connections.

Making better decisions and coping with difficulties should be in line with the total organisation scene or corporate whole. This relies heavily on posing searching questions using the normal why, when, where and how approaches and conceptualising or visualising outcomes.

In practice, typical observations show that there is more reliance on asking searching questions and less on detailed knowledge as senior levels are approached. Also, the more rapid the change the more reliance there is on asking questions and less reliance on experience to seek appropriate solutions. The real difficulty is knowing the right questions to ask.

Character

Nobody possesses all the qualities of character of the ideal supervisor. A compromise is inevitable and the choice will be governed by the particular circumstances.

Some of the important qualities are honesty and trustworthiness, with a strict sense of fairness and justice. A stable personality is essential for an even temper, steadiness and reliability. A direct, open and positive approach is desirable, giving due consideration all parties when dealing with problems and grievances. Cheerfulness and enthusiasm, coupled with a sense of humour, are essential to provide the right type of industrial atmosphere.

In brief, good supervisors must possess something besides technical competence, clearly placing them above their particular group. Someone without higher intellect can still shine by having more drive or inherent qualities of leadership, A person displaying strength of character who 'bubbles over' with activity can make up for other faults.

Each particular combination of qualities suits certain groups in particular work situations. Thus, one person stands out in a group and, provided his or her outlook is reasonably aligned with management policy and not objectionable, he or she is a likely choice.

Selection of supervisors

The importance of careful and fir selection of supervisors is often overlooked by management. Promotions from the shop floor and appointments in the lower levels of supervision are viewed very critically by operatives who are often directly affected.

Poor selection may destroy the efforts of previous supervisors who have managed to improve the industrial climate. Overlooked employees may feel frustrated and suspicious of management if the appointed individual is obviously unsuitable. The working harmony of the group or groups may be upset and resentment tends to spread like a disease - in all directions. The disgruntled individuals, who may have a legitimate complaint, mention the 'injustice' to everyone and a sense of frustration may develop throughout the company.

Some observation on selection

Before considering the methods of selection, some circumstances that can affect selection must be mentioned. A common fault among supervisors is to avoid the promotion of individuals because they are considered to be indispensable in their present positions, even though they are eminently suitable for promotion. Sometimes the supervisor cannot be bothered to train a replacement and the easiest remedy is deliberately to penalise a person's chances of promotion, often forcing the person to seek employment elsewhere.

It is not uncommon for superiors who are able to influence promotion, or who actually select the individual, to allow unimportant incidents to dominate their impressions or opinions of subordinates, sometimes holding a trivial misdemeanour against a person for years. In some cases, even the *suspicion* of wrongdoing is sufficient reason to bypass an individual. A true understanding of reality makes due allowance for human errors and it is wiser and fairer to give other people the benefit of the doubt.

Type suited to management

Managers' opinions on the type of supervisor required are diverse and vary with company size. The manager in a small concern may demand a 'yes man' who carries out orders to the letter; while in a large firm the opposite type may be required, typically one who shows initiative, makes decisions and has a powerful personality. Some prefer the outsider with new ideas; others favour internal promotion. No two managers agree entirely on the qualities they seek for particular position and usually compromise is necessary.

Temperament

Naturally there are many different temperaments that suit a supervisory role, but a certain temperament may suit a particular post. Certainly important general attributes are a stable disposition, reliability and thoroughness. Being able to control emotions in variable circumstances helps greatly when dealing with employees who may exhibit instability or immaturity at times.

Appropriate judgement, perception, sensitivity and intuitiveness are features that highlight potential effective supervisors. What are the best ratios of these four features for a particular post have been the subject of much research.

Methods of selection

The methods of selection can be divided into two

groups to highlight the importance of using scientific methods.

Unsubstantiated methods

All methods that do not allow for systematic selection and result in the detrimental effects of poor selection upon employees and the company come under this heading. These methods do not necessarily imply spontaneous selection - some are planned well in advance - but selection is based not on true grounds but on such grounds as:

- favouritism, promoting friends and relatives
- length of service or age seniority
- high standard of skill alone
- haphazard recommendations by a supervisor
- chance, through stop-gap arrangements, i.e., someone being in the right place at the right time.

Scientific methods

Any method that attempts to reduce the possibility of error comes under this heading. The aim is to find the best person available for each vacancy. All employees, therefore, initially have an equal opportunity and those with ability have good prospects of promotion that will not depend upon influence and favouritism. The essential requirements for any scheme with these aims are as follows:

- planning ahead by estimating the vacancies that are likely to occur

- preparation of a job specification, listing all the main requirements of the vacancy
- advertising internally and externally with the understanding that promotion from within will always take precedence where suitable internal applicants are available
- careful investigation of *all* employees as promotion prospects
- interviews of all candidates who are likely to be suitable, conducted by skilled, objective interviewers and supplemented by appropriate tests
- final choice or approval by top management or a selected panel.

Scientific choice, although not perfect, has obvious advantages. Many factors that may have been omitted are now included in the job specification, there is less chance of potential supervisors being overlooked, better assessment of individuals is now assured and unbiased selection is more likely.

Frankness and open dealings are needed to make the scheme acceptable. Any queries should be discussed openly. Every applicant should be fully informed of proceedings and the unsuccessful candidates must be told why they failed.

A fair scheme must be seen to be fair by everyone. This is essential to smooth the way for the new supervisor, who may have to face special problems if he or she comes from the group to be supervised. This type of change can be a big wrench and it will help the person to adjust quickly if everyone accepts that the selection is fair.

Training and development of supervisors

In the UK this has been neglected for over a century by governments and companies. Insurmountable problems face supervisors and managers unless training is taken seriously. Even when many difficulties are overcome without training, they never know *why* they succeeded. Indeed, conversely, when they fail, they are unable to analyse accurately why this happened and discover their weaknesses.

Training is learning information and skills for the present job; development involves learning not only for the present job but also for future jobs and possible promotion opportunities. This difference in emphasis points at how important it is continually to update knowledge and skills to maintain effectiveness and provide ample opportunity for mental growth.

Informal training

Most supervisors learn their jobs by actually doing them, making mistakes and avoiding making them again as a result of these experiences. Although this system of trial and error is considered to be an essential part of training, practical experience must be supplemented by formal training to form a sound framework for future action.

Working with an effective supervisor is an invaluable experience but, to gain full benefit, a knowledge of the basic elements of supervision helps considerably. Techniques, built up through the experiences of many supervisors and specialists who have spent years studying supervision, need, ideally, to be learned and integrated with informal training.

Formal training

Many of the half a million supervisors in this country have not received *any* formal training, although various of courses have been on offer for a number of years. Any successful training scheme must have suitable training facilities, the right syllabus, appropriate lecturers and back-up staff and strong support from management, who should ensure adequate follow-up and assessment after the course.

Although managers often agree that some form of supervisory training is essential and show enthusiasm when the matter is discussed, few seem prepared to take any practical steps in this direction. Some managers say either that supervisors cannot be spared or that they are too busy to make the arrangements. Others ignore the facilities offered, possibly because they think the subject is unimportant or perhaps they fear that the supervisor, after training, may know more than they do.

The management charter initiative (MCI)

The latest development in formal training for supervisors and managers is the launching of the Management Charger Initiative by the government-funded Training Agency. The aim is to reach agreement on the competences needed by a range of organisations and to classify what the essential knowledge, skills and qualities are. Thus, basic competence standards for education, training and development would be recognised.

Competence - as defined by the Training agency - is the ability to perform activities within an occupational area to levels of performance expected in employment/. A two-part model outlines the competence standards reached by effective managers and the underlying personal abilities and skills required to achieve such standards.

Such standards include managing people, operations, finance and information. Personal competence include displaying self-confidence, taking initiative and coping with stress. The model may be used in many ways and should form the basis for programmes offered by management institutions. These topics have been with us for a long time, but relating the model directly to performance is a new development. A clear distinction is made between courses about knowledge and analysis and those related to competent performance.

Development

This clearly depends on a person's ambition and potential and the seriousness of a company's development programme. Long-term investment is essential in any human resources development scheme, so arrangements must be made and time allowed for supervisors to learn on the job. The process is continuous, with appropriate changes being made along the way to job content, challenges being presented and ample opportunity being given for self-development and initiative.

Comprehensive development schemes are easily recognised. Indications are follow-ups to training, assessing individual requirements, discussing future roles and organisational objectives, stressing conceptual skills development, organisational change, environmental aspects and long-term planning.

Understanding the supervisor's Role

What is a supervisor?

Supervision may occur at various levels of an organisation, but normally on the management level nearest to the workers. Viewed in this way, *supervisors are management representatives who direct the work of operating employees.* They perform management activities such as planning, organizing, staffing, directing, and controlling. Almost without exception they operate face to face with their people to accomplish the work that needs to be done. They are where the action is, surrounded by both problems and opportunities. If an organization's work is to be done at all, they are the ones directly involved in getting it done. Their world is one of action, not idle talk or theory.

The supervisor's unique organizational location

It is sometimes assumed that supervisors occupy a position like that of other members of management, but actually their position is somewhat different, as illustrated by the following chain of command in an organization. The presidents manage a middle-management family, and department heads have a management family consisting of supervisors. The supervisors, on the other hand, head a nonmanagement family of workers. Therefore, they must work on a daily basis with managers above them and nonmanagers below them in the organization.

The supervisory job is further complicated, because there often is a union representing employees. Consequently, a supervisor must understand the union's way of life, its leaders, and how to talk with them. In addition there are personnel representatives, engineers, inspectors, and others that supervisors must deal with on a weakly or daily basis. Together, all of these individuals and groups make a complex situation that is difficult to supervise. As the saying goes, supervisors must wear many different hats as they talk with these various groups. Each has a different outlook and way of thinking, so supervisors need to vary their approaches to fit such difference.

Supervisors are made, not born

Many years ago we thought that supervisors needed to be "natural-born leaders." Unless people were born with the right set of personal characteristics, there was little chance for them to be successful supervisors. Potential supervisors were supposed to have strength of character, dominance, and other apparently desirable personal traits. The trait approach sounded reasonable in theory, but the problem was that it did not prove effective in practice. Successful supervisors exhibited a wide variety of personal traits, so it was impossible to identify any one or two traits that cause effective supervision.

We finally came to realise that success comes to supervisors not because of certain personal traits, but because of certain behavior that is appropriate in supervisory situations. Behavior is the key to supervision, not traits. This means that supervisors are made, not born. Supervision can be taught and learned, so there are plentiful opportunities for many types of people to become successful supervisors. This understanding resulted in an increase in supervisory training programs and improvements in the quality of supervision as supervisors learned more about their role. In short, training combined with on-the-line experience was found to provide the very best supervisory development.

Investment in human resources

The supervisor's principal responsibility is to assure that the organization's investment in human, technical, and economic resources is properly used. Supervisors, therefore, are the ones who help the organization gain a return on its investments. This responsibility applies whether the organization is profit making or not, because all organizations seek high outputs in relation to inputs. To do otherwise would be to waste society's resources, and in these times of scarce resources, waste is not acceptable.

The supervisor's responsibility for investments in human resources is particularly important. engineers can determine how to use an organization's technical equipment, and economists can determine uses for economic resources. however, supervisors can make the most effective use of human resources, because they are the ones in direct, daily contact with employees.

Human resources also have a special characteristic. When properly nurtured, people can grow and develop to become more effective and more capable. It is primary responsibility of supervisors to help their people grow so that they can become more capable persons. In this manner everyone benefits. Employee growth helps the organization, the employees, the society in which we live, and the supervisor. The organization is helped, because employees are able through growth to perform better work. The employees benefit, because they are more fulfilled as persons and can advance in the organization. Society especially benefits because better people make a better society. Finally, supervisors benefit because their employees are doing better work and are more satisfied with their jobs. As a result, human growth is perhaps the most beneficial of all the conditions that supervisors influence.

Key persons in the organizational system

Supervisors are key persons in the organizational system. They represent management to the workers, and they also represent workers to management. Workers know management primarily through their supervisors. Likewise, higher management knows the workers primarily through supervisors. They are an essential element, because they sit astride the chains of authority and communication, and can block almost anything going upward or downward. They make decisions, control work, communicate, lead, and generally play an active part in accomplishing organizational objectives.

Supervisors also bear major pressures of all types, both upward and downward. Workers communicate their expectations to supervisors and expect these ideas to move upward in the system, so that they can get more of what they want. Customers also bring pressures on supervisors for better products and services. In a downward direction, management has specific goals that it wants accomplished, and it brings substantial pressure to see that work is done as planned. management has cost standards, legal restrictions, and other controls that put pressure on supervisors. They also receive pressure from various staff groups who help apply management standards. The result is that supervisors are placed under considerable stress unless they have learned to plan and organize effectively.

A supportive role

Essentially, supervisors perform a supportive role for their people. They try to supply the psychological, technical, and economic support necessary to get the job done. By providing such support, supervisors make the workers' jobs easier, more satisfying, and more effective better training is needed, supervisors help the employees get it. If more security is needed, supervisors try to provide it. They move right down the list of employees' job needs, trying to support all of them. As such, the supportive role is a substantial reversal of the old-fashioned role in which supervisors told employees what to do and they meekly followed. Instead, supportive behavior helps develop cooperation and teamwork in the organization, and supervisors are seen as useful and desirable members of the team because they help groups reach their work goals.

Psychological support for one's group is especially important. Supervisors can provide psychological support because of their face-to-face contact with employees and their control of the immediate work situation. Psychological support is provided through building job satisfaction, improving motivation, providing security for employees, and other similar actions. Such actions require supervisors who are willing to listen to their employees and learn their needs.

Keystone in the organizational arch

Perhaps the concept that best represents the supervisory role as one bearing pressures from both sides is that portraying supervisors as the keystone in the organizational arch. An arch is held together by the keystone that connects both sides and makes it possible for each to perform effectively. The keystone takes the pressure from both sides and uses that pressure to build a stronger arch. The sides can be held together only by the keystone, which strengthens, not weakens, the arch. This keystone position is the important role of supervisors in all organizations.

A related way of viewing the supervisor is as a linking pin connecting workers with the larger organization so that it may operate as a single entity. If it were not for this linking pin, the organisation would be in shambles. Parts would be separated and heading off in their own directions. There would be unity toward common objectives. From these illustrations it is evident that supervisors are crucial links in organizational systems.

Characteristics of the supervisory role

The supervisory role includes a large number of different activities. Supervisors need to have the flexibility and versatility to perform all of these activities, and most of them must be performed well if supervisors are to be effective. We will now discuss various characteristics of the supervisory role, and most of them will be developed further in subsequent chapters.

Leader

Supervisors are first of all leaders. This is their central role. The organization depends upon them to exercise face-to-face leadership in the front lines. Leadership expands and releases the potential that is in people. It creates motivated, willing followers. Top management and staff people can make beautiful plans outlining what should be done, but plans cannot succeed until supervisory leadership at the point of performance releases the powers in people. Thus, leadership is the ultimate act that brings to success all of the potential in an organization and its people.

Leaders need a balanced combination of three types of skills in order to perform effectively. The three are technical, human, and conceptual skills. Technical skill refers to a person's knowledge about various types of equipment and methods. Examples are skills learned by tool-makers, accountants, engineers, and nurses. At the supervisory level technical skill is not as important as it is at the operating level, but supervisors do need some skill of this type in order to be able to communicate with their people and understand their problems. Supervisors who are know-nothings about the technical activities of their departments will have difficulty getting their jobs done.

The leadership role of supervisors particularly requires human skill. It is the ability to interact effectively with people and to build teamwork, and no organization can do without it. Without human skill a team cannot be built, and people cannot be motivated. All supervisors who intend to hold their jobs must be able to work effectively with people.

Finally, supervisors need conceptual skill, because they deal with plans, complex relationships, and other abstractions. They need to be able to relate items A, B, and C in some reasonable pattern in order to understand what is happening in their department. Conceptual skill deals with ideas, human skill with people, and technical skill with things.

Decision maker

Decision making requires the choice of one alternative compared with another, and it is the ever-present stock in trade that supervisors use day after day. Decision making requires a special type of courage. It is easy to study problems once and then to study them again, but it takes courage to decide what to do about them. Decisions require one to take responsibility and to initiate action. These actions invoke risk, because the decision could be wrong, thereby costing the organization money, discouraging employees, or driving away customers.

For supervisors the goal is not to be right all of the time, because that is impossible. A more modest and realistic goal is to be right most of the time, and that is the level of competence that higher management expects of supervisors. An even more important goal is to improve the percentage of right decisions as one gains more supervisory experience. Growth in competence occurs when a supervisor can move from 90 percent right decisions to 92 percent next year and perhaps 93 percent the year after that.

As a matter of fact, the term "right decisions" is somewhat inaccurate to describe what actually happens with supervisory decisions. In real situations, one can differentiate "right" decisions into "good" and "better" decisions.

Planner

Consider the situation of a supervisor by the name of Mabel Morris. Morris is a whiz with people, and she is an expert in the technical side of her office operation. She is a hard worker, arriving before her employees and leaving after they have departed for the day. By many standards Morris is an effective supervisor. Unfortunately, there is one problem, a small item but a significant one in any supervisor's collection of skills. Morris is a poor planner, or perhaps more accurately, she does not plan at all. Her employees try to make up for her deficiencies because they like her, but they cannot do the whole job. The result is that Morris's department is constantly out of schedule with other departments, because it cannot meet its commitments on time. The people in her department are not sure who should do what, or when they should do it. The situation generally is one of confusion, because Morris does not plan.

Planning is essential for total supervisory success. If it is not done well, then other activities are likely to be different because they depend upon accurate planning. Planning is something distinctly different from forecasting. The act of forecasting requires a prediction of the future, but planning organizes knowledge and resources to cause the future. For example, I forecast the weather, and then I plan a hike into the woods based on my forecast of the weather. The future action is based on the plan. Similarly, a supervisor forecasts work requirements for the next week and then plans how the department will get the work done.

A key supervisory planning activity is to set meaningful goals for subordinates. Group members need to feel that they have something worthwhile to do. Without goals, people go off in different directions and begin to lose sight of what the organization s trying to accomplish. The difficulty will continue as long as there is no common understanding of the goals involved.

Organizer

Modern work environments are complex. Organization is the grand strategy to bring order out of chaos when groups work together. Organizing sets the relationships between people, work, and resources. The necessity of organizing - and the havoc of disorganization - are illustrated by disorganizing a short sentence "riirggnagesnotztlsuse." In this form it is nonsense. The parts are not in any meaningful relationship, in the same way that a department can be number of people and resources when it is disorganized. If we reorganise the sentence somewhat, it is workable, but difficult: "organizinggetsresults." By the slight change of converting to a capital "O" and adding two spaces, we achieve a useful, organized sentence : "Organizing gets results."

It is rather easy to see that organising achieves a degree of order in work situations, but there is another part of organizing not so evident. Effective organising is a useful way to bring security and psychological support to one's employees. It does so by helping employees know where they stand and to whom they should go for assistance. when people feel that the organization is set up to serve their job needs, then they tend to feel psychologically supported.

A key part of the organizing job is delegating work to people. When employees accept a delegation, they then become their supervisor's "delegate: or representative. If they do not accept, then delegation has been merely attempted, so delegation also requires behavioral skills to encourage people to accept the responsibilities that are delegated to them. The great advantage of delegation is that it permits supervisors to extend their influence beyond the limits of their own personal time, energy, and knowledge.

Inadequate delegation is a primary cause of supervisory failure. Some supervisors feel that delegation is giving away something, so they psychologically cannot bring themselves to do it for fear that it will weaken them. Others are such perfectionists that they have no confidence in letting others do work for which they are responsible. However, all supervisors need to realize that delegation is the act that makes supervision possible. If there is no delegation to others, there is no one to be supervised.

Sometimes supervisors have to learn the hard way that delegation is a desirable activity. One supervisor had difficulty delegating special reports to his people. He always felt that he could do a better job than they could, so he would not risk delegating a report to them. On one occasion he decided to prove to himself that he could not depend on others to prepare good reports. He assigned a special report to one of his women clerks, but he also worked privately at night on the same report. In this manner he could compare his report with hers to show that he could do better reports than his employees. when her report was received, he had to admit to himself that it was a better report. Having proved his point - but in the opposite of his expectations - he became more free with delegation in the future.

Motivator

An important part of the supervisory job that nearly all supervisors recognize is that of motivator. Motivation is concerned with the human side of supervision rather than the technical side. The basic strategy is to understand peoples' needs and then to relate those needs to the tasks that the organization is trying to accomplish.

The importance of relating human needs to motivational problems is illustrated by a comparison of machine malfunction and operator malfunction. When a machine malfunctions, people recognize that it needs something. Assume that a machine will not grind a piece of metal to a close enough tolerance. Perhaps it needs oil. Or maybe a nut is loose. First the operator tries to find the trouble. Then the supervisor is called. Finally a maintenance mechanic is called, or an engineer, and so on until the cause of the problem is found and the machine is put back into working order. All of the people who tried to find the cause of the machine breakdown did so in an analytical manner based upon their knowledge of the machine's operations and needs. It would have been wasteful to begin haphazardly to tighten nuts and oil gears hoping that the trouble would be corrected. Such action might aggravate the malfunction.

Now suppose that the machine operator malfunctions. Perhaps the operator is not doing an adequate quality of work. The supervisor may feel like taking immediate action without analyzing the situation, but this approach would be no better than haphazard machine repair. Like the machine, the operator is malfunctioning because of particular needs. In the illustration just given, perhaps the operator lack training, or has a conflict with another worker that is upsetting the operator psychologically. When the appropriate problem can be found and corrected, the operator is likely to perform satisfactory work.

Coordinator and controller

It is necessary for supervisors to coordinate and control the complex environment of their departments. Can you imagine, for example, a football play that is not coordinated? People move in the wrong directions or they are in certain places at the wrong times, or both. The result is confusion and a broken play that often causes a loss for the team. The same situation exists with a work environment. The supervisor plays the role of quarterback and is responsible for assuring that all parts of the organisation are working together smoothly.

Control and coordination are closely related to planning, because without plans coordination and control are almost impossible. Consider again the members of a football team. They spend may hours planning their different plays, and then additional hours in practice to be sure that they know how to carry out the plans. Without plans the team would be no more effective than the children's teams that develop spontaneously on playgrounds. They are fun, but they cannot compete with well-planned and coordinated teams. The same situation exists in a supervisor's department. If the supervisor is to be effective, it is essential to develop coordination and control based on sound plans.

Communicator

The importance of communication is made evident by imagining a situation in which supervisors are unable to communicate with their people in any way. The result would be a complete loss of the organization's ability to function. Work could do be done, because people would not know what was needed. Similarly, supervisors would not know what to do, because they would have no feedback from the work situation. The organization would be brought to a complete standstill. Organizations do not face this extreme condition, but many organizations do have such poor communication that there is interference with work performance.

Supervisory plans and ideas, no matter how outstanding they are, become useless unless they can be communicated to employees. Everything that a supervisor does eventually must pass through the bottleneck of communication if it is to reach those involved. Leadership, decision making, planning, organizing, motivating, and all the other supervisory activities require communication before they can take effect. Day-after-day, minute-after-minute, supervisors face a necessity to develop sound communication.

Effective supervisory communication needs to be two-way, upward as well as downward in the organization. The supervisor needs to be an effective receiver of messages as well as sender of them. As a matter of fact, studies show that supervisors usually spend even more of their time listening than they do talking. Consider the process of making a decision. The quality of decisions will depend on the quality of information that supervisors have, and this information is secured by improving inputs from all parts of the organization. Unless supervisors learn from their employees the needs that exist at the work place, the supervisors cannot make effective decisions. similarly, unless supervisors learn what higher management wants done, they cannot make effective decisions. The only way that supervisors can prepare themselves for decision making is to improve their inputs through listening to those both above and below them.

Supervisors are doubly responsible for building communication. First, they are responsible for developing their own proficient communication, as has been discussed. Second, they are responsible for encouraging their subordinates to be effective communicators among themselves and upward to the supervisor and others. In the successful department both the employees and the supervisor are effective communicators. They make up a single team and a single understanding unit that must know what is happening in order to get their jobs done.

From this discussion it is evident that supervisory communication has two broad purposes. First, it provides people the information and understanding they need to do their jobs. But just being able to work together is not enough. People also need suitable attitudes and motivation for working as a team; therefore, the second purpose of supervisory communication is to provide the attitudes for motivation, cooperation, teamwork, and job satisfaction. The accomplishment of both communication goals is required before a supervisor can be successful.

Reward administrator

Another important supervisory activity is that of reward administrator. Supervisors acting as representatives of management provide employees with a proper mix of the rewards available in the organization. There are financial rewards as well as psychological-social ones, such as recognition. Even financial rewards often have overtones of psychological and social value. For example, a raise in pay provides more money, but it also may provide an employee with more status or a greater feeling of accomplishment. Thus, it is impossible for supervisors to separate completely the financial value and the psychological value of rewards.

Supervisors always are interested in getting maximum results from their budget, so they sometimes ask, "Which is more important to employees, financial rewards or psychological-social rewards?" This question is meaningless, because both are important. A more realistic question is how to integrate the two types of rewards so that employees have an effective mix of both.

Supervisors actually administer both rewards and punishments. If a supervisor emphasizes rewards, either financial or psychological-social, then the supervisor is practicing positive leadership. If penalties are emphasized, then the supervisor is applying negative leadership. Most supervisors apply some of both, but the approach that tends to dominate sets the climate in a department.

Negative approaches, such as threats and penalties, do accomplish acceptable performance in many situations, but their human costs are so high that they are not a wise alternative. Negative supervisors act domineering and superior with people. To get work done they hold over their personnel such penalties as loss of job, reprimand in the presence of others, and abusive communications. They display authority with the false assumption that it frightens employees into productivity. These people are really bosses more than supervisors.

Positive supervisors offer encouragement to employees. They give employees motivation to come to work in the morning, because the work is rewarding and satisfying to them. Some of the most important rewards do not cost any budget anything. One of these is recognition. Studies show that workers seek and appreciate it. It is a regular source of feelings of worth and fulfillment. when it is offered genuinely, based on actual achievements, it can be a powerful motivator. Another reward that should not cost any budget is a genuine interest in employees as persons. Employees want to know that they are considered important by supervisors, that supervisors do care, and that supervisors are interested in their problems.

Even the most competent supervisor will at times fall back upon negative approaches, because positive approaches are not always available. However, the historical trend is clearly toward more and more positive approaches to supervision.

Counselor

Another supervisory activity is the counseling of

employees. Counseling has the objective of reducing or removing emotional problems that employees have. As people work together, frictions and problems naturally develop, and it is a supervisory responsibility to reduce these difficulties through counseling. No more complex unit exists than a human being; therefore, it is impossible for a person to be in optimum emotional balance all of the time.

Supervisors need to understand that emotional upsets are not necessarily undesirable or "wrong". Nature gave people their emotions, and sometimes it is more disastrous to suppress an emotion such as anger than to go ahead and express it. But emotional upsets can cause workers to do things that are harmful to their own interests as well as those of the organization. For example, one employee may quit an organization because of some trifling conflict that has been exaggerated until it seems large. In such instances, supervisory counseling may be helpful in retaining employees, thereby helping them as well as the organization. The important point is to channel human emotions along constructive lines rather than destructive ones. Emotions cannot be ignored with the hope that they will go away. They require supervisory efforts just like other parts of the supervisor's job.

When supervisors are working with emotional problems, they are not necessarily seeking the 90-95 percent success rate that is often required in other supervisory actions, such as living within the budget. If only 20 or 25 percent of the employees can be helped, then that is 20 or 25 percent more than would have been helped without counseling, so success has been achieved. However, emotional problems are extremely complex, and supervisors should not expect that they can be easily solved. In many instances, therefore, supervisors will send employees to others such as personnel specialists for counseling.

Trainer

Another activity of the supervisory role is training. Often this activity consumes a substantial portion of a supervisor's time. Training is rewarding both to the supervisor and to employees. If supervisors can develop competent, well-trained employees, then their jobs become easier, because employees can do their work without constant supervision. Employees also are helped. Their self-image and feeling of accomplishment are improved. By becoming better trained they also are more likely to take pride in performing high-quality work. Eventually, training should help them gain wage increases and promotions, because of their added qualifications.

Change agent

A significant activity of supervisors is to administer change in their departments. With the fast technological and social progress that is being achieved in the world, change has become a necessary way life in most organizations. As a representative of management at the work place, supervisors are in the center of the many difficulties caused by change. They need to understand change and how it affects people and organizations. Essentially, their objective is to introduce change with a minimum of upset and in such a way that the organization benefits in the long run. As the saying goes, "Reduce the harm and expand the benefit."

Group participation is an effective way to build support for change. Participation helps employees become involved so that they better understand the change, and it increases their commitment to the change. It assures them that management is not trying to put something over on them by deciding on a change and then imposing it by what is derisively called the "bulldozer" method of change. One special benefit of participation is that it may improve a proposed change by adding contributions from those who will work under it. Participation helps to amend poor plans, and almost always it broadens the supervisor's understanding about the change.

Employee resistance to change is not necessarily bad. In some instances resistance uncovers difficulties connected with the change that were not originally evident to the supervisor. Another benefit is that resistance may cause the supervisor to examine more carefully the negative side effects that accompany change, in the same way that they accompany powerful antibiotic drugs. In other instances resistance causes supervisors to clarify their reasons for introducing change and to define more precisely the desirable results that they expect from change. Resistance also may identify pockets of low job satisfaction and poor motivation in the organization, so that supervisors can take corrective action. Resistance can pinpoint weaknesses in communication, because they frequently arise from inadequate communication about change. And finally, resistance to change can cause supervisors to give more attention to building effective human relations in their departments, because they see that it is necessary to reduce resistance to change.

Other activities

Our discussion certainly has not covered all of the activities that make up the supervisory job, but it has described some of the primary ones. There are others, such as handling grievances, maintaining discipline, providing suggestions for improvements, and creative thinking. The important point is that supervisors have a multitude of different duties requiring a wide variety of skills. supervision is not an activity of one, two, or three skills, but of many skills often quite different from one another. It requires persons who are versatile and capable of understanding complex relationships. They are like jugglers, having to keep many events going at the same time as they work back and forth from one to the other.

A favourable organizational climate

We can sum up the supervisory role by saying that most of what supervisors do is covered by the idea of building a favorable climate for job performance and for the personal growth and satisfaction of employees. The supervisory role exists to carry out organizational objectives, but also to accomplish objectives in such a way that people are rewarded.

A sound climate is a long-run proposition. Supervisors need to take an assets approach to climate, meaning that they take the long-run view of climate as an organizational asset. Unwise supervision, such as threatening and putting pressure on people, may temporarily increase production, but it may so alter the organizatinal climate that the department is in worse condition eventually. The far more effective way is to build a positive climate favorable to performance and personal growth in the beginning.

2 The Development of Supervision

The changing role of the supervisor

Up to the twentieth century, industry was generally considered to be degrading and dirty by the middle and upper classes. Economists concentrated on political economics and business aspects that ignored management. Owners and managers thought managing was an art and, indeed, they were preoccupied with technology, accounts and prices. Consequently supervisors were very powerful, hiring and firing as they wished and receiving little interference from owners so long as profits were acceptable.

During the twentieth century new supervisory roles have emerged and been modified as industrial and economic circumstances have changed. These changes have mainly been due to organised conflict between employees and owners increased competition between countries, two World Wars that demanded higher output and revolutionised technologies, productivity problems, the impact of information technology and the growing importance of organisational culture.

This collective pressure has encouraged the

introduction of various concepts by management pioneers, a growing emphasis on scientific research into behaviour, improved education and training in some countries and increased interest in productivity and design. These features have affected supervisory roles as they have, naturally, coincided with developments and phases of management thinking, descriptions of which now follow.

Autocratic management

During the Middle Ages, supervision through force was commonplace, both for free and slave labour. Output was probably very low and life was cheap.The barbaric use of labour died slowly - slaves were still being used in the British empire even as late as 1833.

Semi-autocratic management

From about 1500 until 1940, a more subtle form of supervision developed. Obedience rested on fear of dismissal, which could mean near-starvation for the worker and his family. Supervisors faced similar treatment as the pool of labour was not being absorbed by industrial growth. This resulted in low wages, cheating and the truck system where workers were paid in goods instead of money or in money but they had to buy their provisions in the employers' shops. This led to organised conflict early in the nineteenth century. By 1940, the bargaining power of the trade unions had strengthened substantially.

At the beginning of the twentieth century, F W Taylor launched new techniques in the USA to foster closer co-operation between management and workers and functionalised many of the foreman's duties. These methods were successful and extensively used to increase production. In Britain, Taylor's teaching was, in the main, ignored.

Constitutional management

The critical war situation in 1940 demanded about four times the existing output from industry. Working overtime did not provide the complete answer to the problem so other ways were tried. Working conditions were improved, welfare officers introduced and joint production committees were established in attempts to increase production.

Disruptions through 'go slows' and unofficial strikes were experienced. Gradually it became clear that the first steps towards maximum efficiency were only likely to be made when human resources and machine operations were considered to be equally important. Close consultation between the government and trade unions led to many trade union leaders and officials entering government departments. Wages were guaranteed and claims were settled at a national level between the unions and employers' associations.

A new era started in the mid-Forties and continued throughout the Fifties of the unions gathering strength and consolidating, with government co-operation and consultation and with employers gradually changing their attitude towards employees.

The concept of a fundamental common interest existing between all groups within a society slowly began to be recognised. Management, however, was viewed as the best-qualified level to pursue these common interests. Opposition from employees was considered to be irrational and misguided, organised by troublemakers or politically motivated fanatics. Supervisors gradually absorbed the ideas of consultation, more emphasis was placed on human relations and loyalty and the 'one big happy family' approach appeared.

The concept is often referred to as the *unitary framework* and, at national level, it includes the idea of acting within the national interest. Thus, anyone, or any organisation, who is construed to be acting against it is considered to be holding the country to ransom or acting in a subversive manner.

Democratic management

In the Sixties, it become increasingly obvious that employees were not responding to the previous approach. Management was forced to recognised that a variety of different and conflicting interests existed and it was assumed that these could,d to some extent, be balanced out through compromises. The employee, therefore, has to surrender autonomy and recognise some rights of management, while management recognises employees' rights to organise, loyally oppose and bargain over procedures and financial rewards.

This *pluralist* approach, benign in character,

became the basis for dealing with industrial relations issues. For the supervisor it meant a change in persuasive techniques, the use of logical argument, even more emphasis on good personal relationships and the encouragement of a free exchange of information.

Contingency management

In the Seventies, several fundamental working assumptions became more acceptable. The pluralist framework became suspect; arising from research the *systems* approach gained support and *contingency* theory developed as a result.

The radical framework

Pluralism failed to account adequately for the marked inequalities and unfair opportunities in society. It could not overcome various fundamental social issues such as an unequal distribution of wealth and a lack of principled basis for income. Among many other criticisms, pluralism wrongly assumed a stable balance of power between employers and employees and, as a result, the *radical framework* became more acceptable on the basis of its analytical power, *not* its political emphasis.

Briefly, the approach goes to the roots of issues and analyses contradictions in social, economic and political structures. Moreover, it locates internal tensions or strains within systems that tend to lead to collapse or adaptation by those who wish to retain basic features. for example, in a culture where freedom, independence, choice and autonomy are important values, conflict is inevitable when most employees are in a work situation that does not agree with these cultural expectations.

From this analysis, conflict is fundamental, has to be expected and taken into account. Co-operation, however, is *also* fundamental in society and industry. Herein lies the basic problem of supervision and management and of organization design, to avoid narrow tasks and the dehumanising of jobs.

The systems approach

In addition to the social aspects, research revealed the importance of technical and economic factors in achieving organisational effectiveness. Consequently new theories viewed organisations as complex systems of individuals, tasks and technology that interacted with, and were part of, a larger environment. Collectively these concepts become known as an *open system*.

Briefly, the systems approach analyses activities to see how they communicate with, and relate to, each other and how they are controlled. Essentially, systems are groups of parts that are dynamically combined and interrelated into a purposeful whole. In other words, to be effective, any collection of activities that has a common objective should ensure that each activity is recognised as having an effect on all other activities, especially when any changes occur.

This simple explanation becomes complex when an organisation is examined. For example, obviously it is pointless for marketing to accept orders that production cannot manufacture. Therefore marketing activities affect production and finance and their effectiveness depends on relating them to other activities to ensure that co-ordination is achieved. Activities that ignore this approach establish boundaries that isolate, cause communication and control problems and defeat co-ordination.

Expanded further, interrelationships operate through complex communication networks that self regulate and adapt to internal and external environmental changes. Networks are examined.

The contingency approach

From systems emerged contingency theory, which determines organisation design and management style for a particular situation. It relies upon finding the best combination or compromise considering the existing or forecasted conditions associated with human skills, technological aspects and the external environment.

This situational approach to management uses all the previous approaches but in the right combination and proportions depending upon circumstances. The supervisor must be knowledgeable, adaptable and able to cope with boundaries problems. Key supervisory roles emerge: achieving co-ordination, encouraging participation, developing group autonomy, recognising situational changes and rapidly adapting to them.

Although this approach is more flexible, changing approaches based upon the situation may confuse subordinates and appear to be inconsistent or insincere. Therefore communicating the reasons for decisions is important. Indeed maintaining certain principles to satisfy moral difficulties and ethics, regardless of the situation, are obviously essential.

Collaborative management

In the late Eighties, productivity difficulties continued. The USA had experienced over 20 years of increasingly strong competition from certain countries, unfavourable economic circumstances, degrees of recession and technological changes. There was a realisation that poor productivity and increasing resentment from employees were caused by the continued imbalance between technical and interpersonal conceptual skills exercised by supervisors.

Proposed restructuring and some actual restructuring have emphasised supervisory role changes. These are based upon introducing or strongly reinforcing existing human resource management. This simply means that managing is concentrated on stimulating employee help and involvement.

Supervisory skills must be balanced to pursue this collaborative philosophy and to cope with the effects on employees of technological change. Since about 1960 writers have expressed concern over the neglect of interpersonal and conceptual skills. Decades ago research findings verified the urgent need, but only recently have the full implications been highlighted through large discrepancies in productivity between competing countries.

The two main features of change in supervisory roles now prevalent were mentioned namely more direct contact with senior managers and modern coaching applied to autonomous teams to develop and employee-centred culture. These are now discussed so that the implications become clear.

Fewer middle managers

Introducing technologies - especially information technology - without appropriate structural change that alters supervisory roles is a serious error. For example, information technology has made desk-top computers commonplace, therefore, ample data are available at all managerial levels. This naturally affects the decision-making process and allows direct access by senior managers to all levels during operations and when information or specialist advice is needed.

This significant change is all-pervading and invites drastic structural reforms. Apart from over-coming many communication problems, the change queries the relevance of middle managers as information processors and as linkages in the organisation. Computerised procedures and systems further reduce the need for information finding, processing and transfer to other levels, which until now were the province of the middle manager.

Already whole layers of middle managers are being removed from many companies. Inevitably supervisors assume these roles as they are next in line. They give information direct to senior levels, hierarchical protocol seems to disappear and new relationships emerge - especially regarding information procedures and systems. Consequently the organisation pyramid is flattened, which simplifies the structure and pushes more power towards the supervisory level. One outstanding example of the imposition of the flatter organisaton concept is the reduction from 11 to 5 levels of management in British Petroleum in 1990.

The remaining roles

Bearing in mind certain organisational principle some middle management roles remain despite recent developments. Typical examples include the following:

- decision making - middle mangers are usually involved in interpretive decision making when structuring decisions are received from senior managers, while supervisors deal with situational decision making.
- middle managers are expected to communicate or talk with the work-force on all managerial matters affecting them, via the supervisors.
- upward communication from the work-force/ supervisors usually flows through middle managers who apply a sifting sorting process.

These three points raise fundamental issues

concerning supervisory roles and responsibilities. Also there is the question of imbalance in the pay structure and the effect on promotion prospects where a large gap appears in the organisation. An interesting feature is how potential senior managers gain experience when middle management levels are removed.

Employee-centred culture

The second feature listed above directly involves employees, who are recognised as being strongly affected by national and organisational cultures.Essentially what is required in this case is to create cultural change so that managers may work jointly with employees and be supportive to the extent of encouraging, tolerating, training and developing, providing appropriate assistance and fostering mutual respect.

This collaborative philosophy is often thrust upon top management once it is realised that it is vital. Previously, strong competition forced companies to streamline the work-force, introduce technological changes in production and encourage employees to be more committed thorough various devices such as co-partnership, profit-sharing schemes and shareholding opportunities. However, such encouragements alone are insufficient to bring about the productive potential of the remaining work-force. Supervisors must play the crucial role of building up employee commitment to the company and achieving more involvement.

Now, collaboration and supportiveness is seen to be the only sensible way to achieve high productivity levels already enjoyed by communities and companies elsewhere.'

Essential guidelines

The following points summarise the concept:

1 recognise and heed the influence of national and organisational cultures.

2 encourage - help people to develop and be tolerant when errors occur.

3 be supportive - always find time to gain employees' confidence by being understanding, ready to listen sympathetically and ensuring that people feel they can express their true feelings in confidence and without fear

4 be responsive to human difficulties and provide appropriate assistance

5 seek ideas and contributions; give due credit

6 demonstrate genuine trust and confidence

7 try to understand and help people in their development and self-development and in solving their personal problems

8 attempt to construct employees' commitment to the company by involving them in discussions and encouraging decision making at their level

9 have strict regard for business ethics and managerial ethics - only fools believe that they can be unethical without other knowing.

National and organisational cultures

Strongly associated with the introduction of an

employee-centred culture is the underrated effect of national culture and prevalent organisational culture. Their deep-seated influence on behaviour should be carefully assessed before embarking on adaptation programmes.

Culture has many meanings. Simplified, it is a way of life, but complex definitions include a particular type, form or stage of intellectual development, all the knowledge, beliefs, customs and skills in a society and the outcome of a specific and unique history. National culture is ingrained in the individual who may be in conflict at work with OC.

The concept of OC as a co-ordinating mechanism means that it includes social interaction, norms, rules and regulations, acceptable physical ad ethical conduct and the degree of group cohesiveness associated with interpersonal and group relations. Further features are the effects of orgnaisational structuring, the impact of fashionable theories that attempt to change OC and attempts to assess OC.

Inconsistencies in company policy

Often overlooked by owners and senior managers is the effect their policies have on OC. Such company culture is often assessed by employees through top management's attitudes towards status, ethical conduct, values and moral codes. The grapevine soon reveals 'behind the scenes behaviour' and typical indicators are salary increases and perks inconsistent with pronouncements for employees, selection scandals, degree of concern for the external environment and manipulation of the law when dealing with injuries, redundancies, takeovers and mergers.

Development of cultural concepts

Effective structuring of a particular organisation hinges on the degree of management competency and the cultural background of its employees. Managers need the capability to adjust and wok effectively within the established OC and to initiate and co-ordinate cultural change.

Views differ on the depth of and the possibility of changing it rapidly. Certainly the complex process involves development of managers, supervisors and all employees to a point where OC evolves to a more advanced form. Another viewpoint is that OC is essentially shallow and short term, so that manipulation of management styles and human resources management have greater impact and national culture is subordinated.

Fashionable theories

Managers may seek short-cuts to success by adopting new theories that claim to solve cultural problems. However a company finds itself with an OC that suits the situation;whether managers have the power to influence OC by changing techniques is debatable.

The use of fashionable theories is encouraged by consultants, business magazines and management courses at colleges. All are useful management tools provided they are in capable hands and used in the right circumstances. Often criticised when they fail to produce forecasted results, they are not necessarily inappropriate - it depends partly on the partiocular organisation structure. Typical theories often quoted are management by objectives, merit rating, critical path analysis, organisation development and quality circles. All are excellent but also often condemned for the wrong reasons.

Assessment difficulties

The role of OC and how it influences behaviour are important features. Often inexplicable employee reactions may be attributed to cultural conflicts at organisational and national levels. Being able to understand and assess culture - which, incidentally, also applies to the supervisor and his or her behaviour - is a difficult task. Intuition, responses by employees and self-examination of the supervisor's own feelings all help, but the assessment's qualitative nature remains.

Further study of this feature is useful. In 1980, Professor Geert Hofstede conducted extensive research in 40 countries on national culture and its effects on employees. He grouped differences in values and bahaviour into four main measures:

- individualism/collectivism
- power/distance

- uncertainty avoidance
- masculinity/femininity

Briefly, the main cultural aspects and their association with particular countries are now given.

Individualism / collectivism

Individualism is the degree of personal choice, freedom and challenges allowed at work, whereas collectivism is a tight social framework that provides security in return for loyalty.

Individualism is preferred in Europe and the USA where self-determination is a strong cultural characteristic. Less well-developed countries tend to prefer collectivism. The Japanese feel that the will of the group should decide beliefs and behaviour.

Power / distance

Power is interpreted as a measure of the degree to which less powerful employees are prepared to accept the unequal distribution of power. *High power distance* accepts low involvement in decision making, typically seen in India and the Philippines. *Low power distance* refers to participative management where employees have a say, typically seen in Denmark and Israel.

Uncertainty avoidance (UA)

This is the extent to which people will tolerate ambiguity and uncertainty and the degree to which they will seek more career stability. Such stability includes rejecting unconventional behaviour and encouraging clear, formal rules.

Germany and Austria have *high UA*, along with Japan, Greece and Portugal, where lifetime employment is a traditional characteristic.

Low UA is seen in the USA, Hong Kong, Denmark and Singapore, where high job mobility is typical.

Masculinity / femininity

Masculinity is taken to mean the extent to which values emphasising assertiveness, acquisition of money and good and displaying little concern for people dominate. *Femininity* is taken to mean the extent to which values emphasising human relationships, concern for others and the quality of life dominate.

High masculinity is seen in Japan and to a lesser extent in the UK, while *high femininity* is noticeable in Sweden and Denmark.

In Japan the combination of high masculinity and high UA seems to produce high motivation where quality circles successfully achieve high quality.

Supervisors' and managers' tasks

Although theoretical definitions of supervisors and managers are clear, the distinction in practice is frequently obscured. A natural tendency to overlap exists, partly from necessity where managers, for example, show a close personal interest to achieve co-operation, and partly from lack of management training. Moreover supervisors are inclined to skip essential detail and concentrate on forward planning; whereas managers are seen to be keen on attending to detail, often to compensate for their lack of drive, vision and decision-making ability. Hence supervisors' and managers' views of each other's jobs vary extensively.

Attempts to overcome this diversity of opinion and operational fault have included retraining managers, completely removing the supervisory level and encouraging collaboration at the interface between supervisors and managers to develop mutual tolerance.

Another factor is the supervisor's organisational background. for example, if a supervisor were promoted from the shop floor or office, the tendency would be to feel a *strong* link with previous peers but a *weaker* bond with management, thus behaviour as a manager may be more difficult. However, starting a job as a junior manager would probably mean a *weak* link with operators or clerks, but a *strong* link with management. Thus it may be easier to act as a junior manager but more difficult to relate to employees.

Improving relationships

In both instances, the void between managers and employees is clearly marked and somehow interface difficulties have to be tackled. Bringing the two sides together involves various techniques. Three typical approaches are collaboration, retraining and the classless concept.

The collaborative approach

As already noted, collaboration means sharing problem solving and decision making, communicating views and ideas *on an equal footing*. The aims must be clear:

- to close up the structure
- to analyse and arrive at more acceptable approaches
- to improve relationships generally.

The retraining approach

This means developing both parties to understand the two environments thoroughly—the management sphere and the working sphere. forgetting traditions, changing basic attitudes and ideologies and achieving co-operation are a part of the programme.

The classless approach

This concept attempts to remove the variety of class structure models in organisations. Many countries are proud of their 'classless' society. In the UK, despite Prime Minister John Major's dreams of a classless society, many mangers seem to be proud of belonging to a seemingly different class, are preoccupied with status and intent on widening rather than closing the gap. Senior managers even consider themselves to be upper class. Seldom do managers see themselves as part of the proletariat even though they are being employed by the company. Supervisors, though, seem to feel that the divide is a level above them.

The damage to relationship often involves mental—and sometimes physical—reactions against those who think themselves above everyone else

3 The Supervisor's Job and Supervisory Training

The key to success for any organization is good management, and the key man in good management is the supervisor.

If you stop to think for a moment, you will see why this is true. For a firm to be successful, the employees must produce a quality product at a high level of efficiency and at a low cost. Unless this is done, all fancy footwork, knowledge, and actions of upper management mean nothing. Until employees fill out reports, attend to patients, assemble parts, type letters, test products, load trucks, wait on customers, dig ditches, take inventories, or do whatever needs to be done—and do it efficiently and effectively—then all the *top* management skills that the organization possesses will not make it successful. Instead, it is the *first-line* supervisor who is responsible for seeing that work is accomplished. And unless he does his job well, the entire managerial pyramid will be weakened. In fact, it may even crumble and fail.

Good supervision, in fact, is just about the single most important factor in the success of our American economy. It is responsible for more than doubling our national output during the past twenty years. Because of good supervision we have produced a staggering array of new products, new homes, new automobiles, new clothing, new tools, new TVs, and so on. How, you might ask, have good supervisors done all this? The answer: they have done it by wisely directing the efforts of others, by wisely using the manpower available to them, and by wisely putting the right combination of men and materials together to get work done. *The key to success for any firm is good supervision.*

What is the supervisor's job?

Supervisors are known by different names in different companies. A supervisor might be called either a foreman or fore lady, a leadman, a section chief, a front-line supervisor, a floor chief, a section head, or a department head. Whatever he is called, a supervise must be able to understand people, be able to motivate them, be an energetic leader, be a good planner and allocator of work, be wise and just in making decisions, be knowledgeable about technical aspects of the work, and finally, be able to serve as an effective liaison between top management and the workers. All this sounds like a description of a superman - and it is! Most of us do not have all these attributes and capacities; therefore, we need to study what the supervisor does and how he does it so that we can grow in that direction - so that we can develop our capacities to the point where they meet the needs of a good supervisor.

Supervisors' jobs vary widely in their

complexities. One foreman may be responsible for supervising a move gang whose duty is to load and unload trucks at the loading dock. He may do little more than tell the crew what to load into a truck and where to put material being taken out. Basically, he sees what needs to be done and tells his men what to do. Notice we said, *tells his men what to do*. This is what supervision is all about. *Supervisor get things done through the efforts of other people,* Supervisors, then, accomplish the objectives of the organization by directing the efforts of others.

Some supervisory jobs, of course, are much more complex than the loading and unloading job described above. A complex supervisory position may require a full knowledge of computer operation and application, a full knowledge of health services, a vast comprehension of consumer needs and wants, and the issuance of directives to skilled men with advanced educations. But, while this job is more complex than the loading job, the supervisor's part is still the same: *getting things done through the efforts of others.*

How many supervisory levels are there?

As indicated previously, a supervisor is a manager who gets things done through the efforts of other people. This description of a supervisor holds true regardless of the level on which he operates.

Most of the time you hear people speak of top-level supervisors for managers, middle-level supervisors, and first-line supervisor. *Top level supervisors* are the big bosses in charge of the whole operation. The president of a corporation is a top-level supervisor. The administrator of a hospital is a top-level supervisor. A person in charge of a plant - a textile mill, for example - is a top-level supervisor, as is the owner-manager of a small firm. In each instance, the person holding down the top job is a top-level supervisor.

Middle-level supervisors are higher up than first-line supervisors but below the top-level supervisor. A department manager in a retail store who has several supervisors working for him would be a middle-level supervisor. A person in charge of purchasing or production for a business would be a middle-level supervisor. His title might be Director of Purchasing or Production Manager.

First-line supervisors are the key men in the managerial family who carry out the policies and directives of middle and top management through face-to-face contact with the workers. Middle management's directive are carried out by first-line supervisors through the efforts of the nonsupervisory work force, the workers.

What does a supervisor do?

If we were to follow a supervisor about all day and list everything he does *as a supervisor,* the list would probably look something like the following:

- Talks to employees
- Gives directions to employees
- Dictates letter
- Sets production or sales goals
- Hires new employee

is used to set the points on a gasoline engine? To be a good supervisor, therefore, you will need to have the technical skills necessary to understand the processes and equipment used. In many instances, these technical skills are acquired through on-the-job training or through vocational programs.

In addition to these technical skills, a supervisor needs *human* skills. Human skills are those skills that enable a supervisor to build cooperative efforts within the group he leads. A human skill primarily concerns working with *people,* whereas a technical skill primarily concerns working with *things*

Human skills involve being aware of your own feelings, beliefs, and attitudes about others. By being aware of himself, a supervisor with good human skills can *understand* and *accept* the beliefs and attitudes of others and recognize that they many differ from his. By understanding and accepting the beliefs and viewpoints that differ from his own, a supervisor will be more skillful in understanding what others mean by statements and their actions. Recognizing these differences, a supervisor can do a better job of communicating ideas to others. A supervisor, for example, may not be in favor of having a union in the company. Most of his employees, however, may be in favor of having a union represent them. Knowing and understanding his employees' feelings about unions and why they want to be represented by them, the supervisor can create an atmosphere of understanding in which employees can freely discuss unionism - an atmosphere in which they feel free to express their ideas without fear of ridicule. With human skills, a supervisor is sensitive to the motivations and needs of others an can judge the probable effects various courses of action may have on his employees. With this human skill, he can take actions that will tend to promote harmony and good effort within the group.

Human skills should be so much a part of a supervisor that he applies them continuously. Even when a foreman is not directly supervising his employees, everything he says or does will have some effect on them, because what he does will reflect his true self to his men. Human skills, therefore, should not be thought of as techniques you can apply or use at will. To the contrary, a good supervisor should have developed human skills that are so much a part of him that they cannot be separated from him. Most of us know people who don't have good human skills. They are the ones who always seem to open their mouths and put both feet in. They rub others the wrong way. The supervisor who tells an employee, "I don't want to know why you are late; whatever your excuse, if this happens again, you'll be fired" doesn't have good human skills.

Finally, a supervisor needs *conceptual* skills. Conceptual skills are those that enable a person to visualize something in its entirety. A person with good conceptual skills can "see" and understand all parts of a business and how each part contributes to the whole organization. He understands the role that accounting plays; how purchasing, sales, and finance relate to accounting; how personnel is a part of the total concern; how personnel function relative to each of the other divisions or parts of a firm; and so on. A supervisor with conceptual skills can visualize the part that the organization plays in the social, economic, and political forces in the community, state, or region. A supervisor needs conceptual skills so that he can make wise decisions. With good conceptual skills, he can make wiser decisions, because he will have the capacity to consider the impact that a certain decision will have on all parts and functions of a firm. He will understand the part that a wage increase would play in the total business. He can see, for example, that a 10% wage increase would have a bearing on production costs, morale, the selling price of the product, consumer acceptance and purchase of the product, profit, and the long-run chances of success for the firm in the community—to name a few.

With good conceptual and human skills, a supervisor will be able to visualize the effect that would result from giving a relatively new employee a choice job on a new machine. It may cause discontent among other employees, unrest, a possible labor slowdown or stoppage, loss in product quality, decrease in morale, and so on. You can easily think of other possible influences.

A good supervisor, then, needs these three skills: *technical* skills so that he can understand and perform the technical activities required, *human* skills so that he can both motivate others and understand individual feelings and actions, and *conceptual* skills so that he can clearly understand and coordinate all the activities of the firm through wise decision making. Technical skills are probably in greatest need in the lower levels of a firm. Human skills, on the other hand, are in real need throughout every level of the firm. Conceptual skills are more critical at the higher levels of the firm.

What functions does a supervisor perform?

Supervision deals with getting things done through the efforts of others, Supervisors tell other employees what to do. As was previously indicated, supervisors can also perform some job - such as running a machine. While running the machine, of course, he is not supervising but is performing some work. To achieve his job of getting things done through the efforts of others, every supervisor engages in several functions or acts.

1. He must plan his work and establish objectives. This is called the *planning* function.
2. He must organize people and materials in order to co-ordinate activities and actions. This is the *organizing* function.
3. He must secure qualified personnel to do the work - the *staffing* function.
4. He must direct the efforts of his employees - the *directing* function.
5. He must control the activities of his employees - the *controlling* function.

Let's look at each of these functions and see why a supervisor needs to perform them.

Planning. A plan is a course of action to accomplish something - like a plan for a family vacation. Planning is the process involved in developing and formulating the course of action needed to accomplish your objective. Planning is not a function reserved just for top and middle management alone. To the contrary, first-line supervisors are also actively engaged every day in planning - though their planning may not be as complex or extended as far into the future as top-level planning. However, without this planning by the supervisor, his department's activities may well become disorganized, confused, and ineffective. In fact, thoughtful and careful planning by a supervisor can do much to change him from a mediocre supervisor to an outstanding one ready for promotion to a bigger job.

Organizing. Organizing consists of:

1. Determining what activities need to be accomplished to get the job done.
2. Grouping and assigning these activities to employees.
3. Giving the employees the necessary authority to carry out the activities in a coordinated manner.

All supervisors perform this function, though those at the top level are interested in the broader aspects of the firm, while the first-line supervisor is interested in organizing his own department so that work can be accomplished in the best way possible.

Staffing. The staffing function consists of those activities needed to recruit, hire, and retain individuals to fill jobs in the firm. In some companies, this is done by a personnel department; in some it is a joint responsibility shared by the supervisor and the personnel department; while in other companies, it is the full responsibility of the supervisor.

Directing. Directing deals with influencing, guiding, or supervising subordinates in their jobs. It consists of telling them what to do. It involves a large amount of communication and, in most supervisory positions, consumes the greater part of a supervisor's workday.

Controlling. The essence of control from a supervisory standpoint is, simply, that a supervisor must control people. If people are controlled properly, then actions and events will conform to plans. In essence, control is the check-up part of managing.

What are a supervisor's responsibilities?

In the past, many people felt that a supervisor had only one responsibility—making money for the business. Today, however, smart managers are developing a new sense of supervisory responsibility. Some people call it *business statesmanship*. Others call it *enlightened leadership*. Whatever its name, it refers to the fact that business leaders are beginning to realize that they have responsibilities not just to the owners, but to many other groups both inside and outside the firm. Today good supervisors recognize a sense of responsibility to the community as well as to the people inside the plant. They recognize their responsibility to their owners, their employees, their customers, the general public, and the government. Let's look at each of these briefly.

Responsibility to Owners. As owner invests in a firm to make money. Perhaps more than anything else, the owner wants a good return from his investment, along with some security. He will, of course, agree that his company should treat its employees fairly and that it should be honest with the public and its customers, but primarily he wants dividends, and dividends can only come from profits.

A supervisor's responsibility to the owner of the business, then, is to operate his department in such a manner as to give him the highest *long-run* return on investment. Working for the highest long-run profit will never conflict with obligations that a supervisor has to other individuals and groups. For example, an extensive program to construct new buildings and purchase new machinery may materially reduce profits for several years, but in the long run, profits would be greater than if the new programs were not undertaken. In fact, without the new building program, the business might lose its competitive advantage and fail.

Responsibility to Employees. An enlightened supervisor also recognizes that he has a very definite responsibility to his employees. Even as stockholders have invested their money, so have employees invested their time, their energies, and their efforts with a firm. Having thus cast their lot, employees are entitled to having a farsighted supervisor who recognizes his specific responsibilities to them as well as his responsibility for operating his department in a profitable way.

A supervisor is responsible to each employee for giving him a courteous reception upon starting to work and for placing him in a position for which he is qualified by abilities and interests. Inasmuch as employees spend about 50% of their waking time at work, supervisors are responsible for providing physical facilities that meet accepted standards of cleanness, light, heat, ventilation, and safety. In addition to these physical aspects, supervisors are responsible for providing leadership that will inspire employee cooperation and allow them to work in a relaxed manner, confident that their best interests will be served.

Supervisors are also responsible to their employees for planning the work of the department so that a *steady* job will be provided. This may call for intricate planning of seasonal work, but the benefit to the employee and the community is obvious.

Finally, supervisors are responsible for increasing the day-by-day satisfaction and well-being of their employees in relation to their work, their fellow employees, and the company. This responsibility is incorporated with the obligation to provide the opportunity for advancement and promotion within the limits established by the size and nature of the organization. It incorporates a moral responsibility to train employees so that they can attain the highest level of responsibility of which they are capable. And it includes the responsibility to recognize and respect the individual dignity of men - to treat each worker as an entity and not as an impersonal part of a group of humans.

While the above list is not all-inclusive, it will give you some idea of the many responsibilities that enlightened supervisors feel toward their employees.

Responsibility to customers: A supervisor's basic responsibility to the customer is to help the company make a quality product that the customer wants, when and where he wants it, at a price he is willing and able to pay—and all at a fair profit. In addition, the supervisor is responsible to the customer for building integrity into the company's products—for striving to improve the company's products so that they represent better buys for the customers and incorporate the company's reputation for fair and responsible treatment.

Responsibility to the public and government: Business exists because the public and the government allow it to exist. Corporations come into being and are allowed to operate because the citizens and the government of a particular state *agreed* that they could do so. Business owns property and locates buildings in accordance with the rights *granted* by local governments. Because a business exists and operates through the consent of the public and government, it has a very definite responsibility to each.

To help meet these responsibilities, a supervisor should first of all obey the operating laws set forth by the local, state, and federal governments. This supervisory responsibility includes obeying not only the letter of the law, but the spirit of the law as well. Where as law is vague and loopholes exist, the supervisor is responsible for operating within the total meaning of the law, considering the best interests of his employees and the community.

Many of the supervisory responsibilities discussed here were not recognized twenty years ago. Today, however, enlightened managers are developing an awareness and a philosophy of their multiple obligations and responsibilities. Managers are recognizing as never before that a firm will not prosper for any considerable time if its sole objective is to make as much money as quickly as possible.

What qualities do you ned to be a successful supervisor?

The characteristics or qualities that make a supervisor successful are difficult to pinpoint precisely. Some are more important than others and some are difficult to describe. However, we do know that a successful supervisor must be able to inspire his employees, motivate them, and direct their work. As previously indicated, he needs to have technical, human, and conceptual competence. In addition to these qualities, you will also need to have an open mind. You must learn to search outside the everyday rut for a better method, a new policy, in improved way of doing things. You must, in other words, always be open to suggestions for a better way of performing any task.

A good supervisor needs to be able to discover what the problem is in times of trouble. Many people don't have this ability; they simply cannot see what is wrong when trouble erupts. They see and treat the symptoms of the problem rather than the causes of the problem. They may give aspirin for a headache, when the real problem and cause of the headache is eyestrain. The cure, therefore, is to purchase glasses—not aspirin. Thus, a good supervisor needs to have the ability to get to the heart of the problem, to discover its real cause, and to take action to *cure* the trouble.

To do a good job, supervisors also need most of the following qualities. See how many you have, and make plans to develop those in which you are weak.

1. *A good supervisor should have ambition - the desire too manage and grow.* He should always be willing to learn, to develop new skills, to broaden his job. He should not be afraid to take a chance but instead should possess confidence that he will succeed.

2. *A supervisor should be a self-starter:* He should think and move on his own initiative, and not wait to be told by others to do something. To do this he needs self-confidence and courage to move ahead.

3. *A supervisor should be able to think:* This is perhaps the hardest task most people face. Most of us find it easy *to do, to act, to perform.* We have difficulty, however, in thinking clearly about a problem - our minds wander, we are distracted by noises or other problems, or we prefer to *do things* rather than *think* about how to solve problems.

4. *A Supervisor should be able to express himself clearly:* The best idea in the world is worthless unless it is communicated well. As you know, supervisors spend most of their time communicating; therefore, they need to do it well. We aren't talking about great speaking or great writing. What we are talking about instead is the simple ability that a supervisor needs to get ideas across clearly to his employees so that they can understand what he wants them to do.

5. *A supervisor should be a salesman:* Any idea that you think up and communicate to others still needs to be "sold." Selling an idea - convincing others of its worth - is one of a supervisor's prime tasks. Selling a plan of action to others is a vital part of communication and motivation by supervisors.

6. *A supervisor should possess moral integrity:*

Truthfulness, honesty, and integrity should be so much a part of a supervisor that his subordinates will have confidence in him and his actions.

7. *A supervisor should be able to organize:* This is another very important attribute, because a supervisor is constantly called on to organize his own work as well as the work of his men in order to maximize output.

9. *A supervisor should have the ability to work with and through other people:* He has to be able to get along with others and to get them to do what needs to be done for the organization.

10. *A supervisor should be willing to tackle and make tough decisions:* Anyone can made an easy decision, but a good supervisor must be willing to tackle the hard problems and make tough or unpopular decisions.

11. *A supervisor should be dynamic and have the ability to inspire others:* This is that special something, which you can't put your finger on, that makes you want to follow the directions of and work with some leader.

12. *A supervisor should have the ability to size up others and recognize individual strengths and weaknesses:* This is a critical ability needed by supervisors in order to get the right man in the right job, as well as reject the unqualified applicant.

13. *A supervisor should like people:* He should like

to be with people and work with people. In fact, it is hard to visualize a supervisor who doesn't like his men, who doesn't have a sense of loyalty and feeling for his employees.

14. *A supervisor should be a balanced person:* This means that he should be levelheaded, understanding, firm, able to laugh, and fair.

Are any special qualities needed?

Yes. In addition to the characteristics and qualities discussed previously, you will need to possess, if you want to be a good supervisor, a *willingness to subordinate your own desires and wishes* to those of *your* supervisors and bosses. You'll have to realize that you cannot have your own way over every matter but must instead submit to your boss's wishes.

Despite all that can be done by you and others, disputes, grievances, and problems will arise among employees. In each instance, you will need to call on every ounce of *levelheadedness and wisdom* that you possess to mediate these situations and render fair and impartial answers to the petitions.

You will, of course, need to have a thorough *understanding of what your job is* and what you are supposed to do. Knowing the technical aspects of your job will give you confidence and assurance in dealing with problems and in talking with employees.

You will need to *win the friendship, loyalty, and support* of your employees as well as your other associates. In addition, you will need to possess and show a spirit of willing cooperation with other supervisors in your division as well as other areas of the firm. No man is an island. You live and work with others, and to succeed as a supervisor, you will need all the help you can get from your associates.

You will need *a good mind and a good education.* A good mind is reflected in an open and willing-to-learn attitude. You don't mind tackling problems. A good education is reflected not in the number of years spent in school, but in the quality and amount you absorbed. Experience in many instances can compensate for formal education. You will need to get along well with your associates and employees—a quality that we learn from experience rather than schooling.

As a good supervisor, you should always try to *see the whole picture* in order to understand what top and middle management wants done and why. To be a successful supervisor, you will need to understand the whole picture and communicate this in an understandable way to your fellow employees.

Patience is a virtue that you will need to be successful—patience to listen to and understand employees; patience to spend whatever time is needed to understand and improve work situations and worker relations; patience to take the time necessary to plan the total work flow and organize it in such a way that employees will feel comfortable in doing their jobs.

To be a successful supervisor, will need to be *flexible* in order to adjust to new procedures, new and changing conditions, and new ways of solving problems. Resisting change is one of the surest ways to slow down progress. Successful supervisors are the ones with open and receptive minds who do not resist change. They welcome new ideas, new ways of performing old jobs, and new concepts about how things can be improved.

Finally, and perhaps most important, you will need to possess *initiative* and the *desire to succeed*. If your desire to be a successful supervisor is strong enough, you may well overcome any shortcomings that you see in yourself. Determination, willingness, and the strong desire to be a successful supervisor will put you well on the way to achieving your goal.

Perhaps as you think back over what has been said, you may wonder how you can develop all of these capacities. The answer lies in hard work, motivation on your part, and in formal and informal education. Managerial or supervisory courses will help in many instances. Experience can also teach you if you will allow yourself to profit from it. Another way to learn that has been used by a lot of successful men is to watch good supervisors at work. Observe what they do, how they handle difficult employees, how they solve though problems. Learn from their good as well as their poor habits. Accept and model your actions after their good habits, but reject their poor behavior patterns.

One of the most successful supervisors that I ever worked for had no formal education in the area of human relations and supervision. He didn't know what anthropology or sociology was. He finished high school and immediately started working and learning from the school of hard knocks. He worked hard and possessed many of the characteristics talked about above. A few years after starting work, he was promoted to a supervisory position. As a supervisor, he was well-liked by his men; they could always count on his going to bat for them and getting a fair decision. He got along well with other managers and earned their respect and admiration. His employees could always be sure that he would recognize and reward hard work and talent, and they could always count on his being available to hear out a problem or mediate a tough decision. He was no patsy or easy pushover, but he did welcome the discussion of ideas that were at variance with his men. He was, in fact, one of the smartest, hardest-working managers I have ever known. And he developed into this position through extra effort and desire. If this is your objective, there is no reason why you, too, cannot succeed if you work hard enough at it.

Are there opportunities in supervision?

The opportunities in supervision are innumerable. Virtually every business enterprise, every governmental office, and every institution presents possibilities for the application of supervisory skills. Every business is a potential source of employment for you. Because their worth and contributions to a going concern are recognized, young men and women who qualify as potential supervisors are being sought by business today as never before.

As indicated in this chapter, you cannot be a supervisor by simply deciding to be one. A great deal of study, hard work, on-the-job training, and preparation are necessary in many instances. Developing into a supervisor, therefore, is a long but rewarding process. The field offers abundant opportunities for self-expression and financial reward to those who are willing and can qualify. You can if you will.

Supervisory management

Very few organizations are satisfied with the performance of their first-level supervisors and foremen. Research conducted at the University of Wisconsin Management Institute indicates that foremen and supervisors are from 50 to 65% effective—as evaluated by middle-and top-management people. The main reasons for such limited effectiveness are that they do not have:

1. a clear understanding of what is expected of them.
2. the proper attitude and motivation to do their best.
3. the knowledge and skills that are necessary to do the job.

Which of these causes for inadequate performance can be corrected by effective training and development?

The first one, not understanding what's expected, is a communication problem - not a training problem. It can be corrected only by clear and complete communication between supervisor and his boss. The second condition, poor attitude or lack of motivation, can be improved through training and development. Likewise, the third - lack of knowledge and skill - is clearly a problem that can be corrected by effective training.

Improving performance on present job—as it now exists

Training and development can be important in improving the performance of foremen and supervisory in their jobs as they now exist. Attitudes, knowledge, and skills can all be improved. Such improvement can change the job behavior of supervisors, thus producing better performance and results.

Recently, I conducted a short training course for foremen and superintendents of a small Wisconsin shoe manufacturer. The objective of the program was to reduce turnover and the main focus was on effective induction and training of new employees. At the end of the program, we evaluated by asking the participants for their reactions. They were less than enthusiastic. Typical comments indicated that "the ideas that Kirkpatrick expressed were good but they don't agree with the way things are done here"

These reactions prompted a research study in which I was asked to interview each of the foremen to determine his attitudes toward the company as well as his recommendations. In the personal interviews I asked four questions:

1. How do you feel about your job?
2. How do you feel about the company?
3. What are your main problems in doing your job?
4. What suggestions do you have for improvement in the company?

Well, I got an earful of complaints and gripes about many aspects of the company. They reflected a general feeling of frustration and low morale on the part of the foremen. The negative attitudes of these foremen are probably reflected in the attitudes and performance of their subordinates, the workers. Therefore, it was most important that the attitudes of these foremen, as well as their knowledge and skills, be improved in order to improve the morale and productivity of the workers.

After I completed the interviews, I have the company executives a report. They began to take steps to correct the policies, procedures, and practices that were causing poor supervisory attitudes.

This example illustrates several points about supervisory training and development:

1. The attitudes of the foremen and supervisors can have a significant impact on the effectiveness of the program. I'm sure that my ideas and recommendations were not accepted by the foremen of the shoe manufacturing company because of existing management policies and practices that had created low morale on the part of the foremen.

2. Negative attitudes of supervisors must be changed if the workers are expected to improve performance and increase productivity.
3. Negative supervisory attitudes can't be corrected in the classroom if they reflect unsatisfactory job conditions such as low pay, inadequate work force, poor management policies, delays in getting raw materials, excessive pressures to produce, etc.

The main thrust of supervisory training and development should be to improve the performance of a supervisor on his present job. Present attitudes, knowledge, and skills can be improved and immediate payoff can be obtained in improved performance and productivity of the workers they supervise.

Improving performance on present job as it will exist

A second need for training and development exists if the job of the supervisor and foreman is changing with changes in the organization. The content of this training should include both the technical and managerial aspects of the supervisor's job. In the technical area, a supervisor may need to learn more about equipment, machines, tools, quality control, time study, the labor agreement, raw materials, manufacturing processes, and other technical subjects related to his job and his department. The managerial aspects may include the latest and best approaches in such areas as motivation, decision making, and management by objectives.

Preparing for advancement

If the present supervisor or foreman is being considered for higher level positions, new training needs emerge. These, of course, are related to the job of middle management instead of first-level management. The technical needs may include increased understanding of the computer, linear programming, PERT Program evaluation and review technique, and budgeting. The managerial needs might include organization development, manpower planning, delegation, styles of leadership, decision-making, and long-range planning. These are in addition to more in-depth understanding of motivation, communication, and the development of his subordinates.

Summary

There are three main reasons why supervisory training and development are worth the time and money they cost. First of all, if the supervisor's present performance is not as good as it can be, training can improve his attitudes, knowledge, and skill, and increase his effectiveness and that of his department.

Secondly, the jobs of most supervisors and foremen are changing. Therefore new knowledge - technical and managerial—must be acquired in order to effectively perform the first-level management job as it will be.

Finally, some supervisors and foremen will be promoted to middle-management jobs in the near future. Training and development can prepare them for effective performance of the job when the promotion occurs.

Time and money spent on supervisory training and development should be considered an *investment* and not an expense. It is an investment in the future of the organization, recognizing that people are an organization's most important asset. Benefits should be viewed as a return on the investment. The extent of the benefits will depend on many of the factors that will be covered in this book. Benefits to the supervisor can include improved attitudes, knowledge, skill, performance, and rewards. Benefits to the organization can include increased productivity, reduced costs, reduced turnover, and greater profitability.

Who is responsible?

Three different people in an organization can be held responsible for the training and development of a supervisor. These are: (1) The supervisor himself, (2) his boss and (3) a staff man.

The supervisor himself

It is generally agreed that each supervisor has responsibility for his own development. Some supervisors have accepted the *entire* responsibility and have laid out their own program for self-development. However, the majority of first-level supervisors have not taken the initiative in planning and implementing their own program of self-improvement. Therefore, it is no practical for most organizations to adopt the philosophy that development is the *sole* responsibility of the supervisor himself. He needs stimulation and assistance if improvement is to take place.

The boss

It is a well-accepted principle that every boss is responsible for the development of his subordinates. This certainly seems logical: the boss is responsible for the performance of his subordinates and that performance depends largely on their training and development. Nearly every job description for department head, superintendent, or other middle-management job spells out the responsibility for training and developing subordinates, with particular emphasis on the subordinate's present job.

The staff man

In larger organizations, there is usually a person whose job is training director, manager of management development, or some other title which includes the words "training" or "development." These people usually have a responsibility for the training and development of all management personnel. In smaller organizations, responsibility for the training and development of supervisory personnel may be assigned to the personnel manager or some other staff man.

Responsibility versus authority

Is there a conflict among the responsibilities of these three different people? There need not be. All three of them can share the responsibility and improve the chances that the supervisors and foremen will be trained and developed.

The supervisor himself

The fact that a supervisor has much of the

responsibility for his own development does not necessarily mean that he also has the authority for it. For this does not mean that he can do whatever he wants to in order to improve himself. On his own time, of course, he has the authority to attend a seminar, read a book, or take a Dale Carnegie, Evelyn Wood, or correspondence course. However, he would not have the authority to spend the company's money or to take a working day off to attend a seminar he feels will help him develop.

The boss

The boss, on the other hand, has more authority. He can send the supervisor away for a week to attend a seminar on company time. He can assign him a book to read and check to be sure he reads it. He can give the supervisor special job assignments in order to improve his knowledge and skills. He can set up an internal training program and pull the supervisor off the job to attend it. In other words, he has the authority to tell his subordinate what to do and when, and can probably commit company money and time.

The staff man

The staff man has no authority over the training and development of supervisors. In fact he has responsibility without any authority. He has to sell his ideas to the boss as well as to the supervisors themselves. His success in meeting his responsibility depends on his ability to sell himself, his philosophy, and his program.

The role of the staff man

Let's consider four possible approaches that the staff man can use. He can:

1. Provide whatever help the line manager requests.
2. Help the line manager determine the training needs of his department and help him develop a program to meet these needs.
3. Develop an effective training program and sell it well enough so that the line manager will want it.
4. Develop an effective training program and gain enough status and power so line management will not dare disapprove.

Let's look at these four possibilities one at a time.

Provide help as asked

This is a fine approach, especially if line managers are training-oriented. If enough line managers are desirous of help, the staff man does not need to do any selling; he will be kept busy providing training help as requested. The staff man must be sure that the training is effective, and if he can't do the whole job himself, he must enlarge his department to get the job done. Line managers will back him up in his request for an assistant because their needs are not being served.

Assist in determining and meeting needs

This approach can also be very successful. It is partly selling and partly providing help as asked. The staff man should stimulate the line manager to think about his problems and help him to determine which problems can be solved by training activities. The staff man is helping the line manager solve problem. In so doing, the staff man must communicate and sell his training know-how and capabilities to the line manager. There is no pressure on the line manager. He will use the staff man's help only if he feels it will help him meet his objectives without costing too much time or money.

This approach requires a staff man with three strong qualities.

1. A through knowledge of training principles, approaches, and available resources.
2. Salesmanship.
3. The ability to follow through and deliver a quality program.

A staff man with these qualifications can be very successful. Some line managers are willing to give this kind of a staff man a try. If he can deliver, they will be pleased and will probably ask for more. Also, one satisfied line manager will tell another that it is a good training program. And as long as the line manager is convinced that the staff department is providing a service that is worth the time and money, the staff man will be successful in fulfilling his responsibility to see that effective training is being done.

Develop a training program and sell it

The success of this approach depends on the staff man's ability to plan or purchase a training program and to sell it to line management. In developing the program, the staff man should be sure that it meets the needs of the supervisor. One of the best ways is to involve line managers in the decisions related to the program. For example, several alternative proposals can be made to line managers and the decision left to them. Or the staff man can recommend and sell a specific program that he is confident will meet the needs. Obviously, a history of successful programs will make it much easier to sell programs to line supervisors. Therefore the staff man should do a thorough job in planning programs that he knows will be effective.

Develop a training program and fore acceptance

Some staff people are able to carry out their training responsibility by enjoying the status and power which makes line managers reluctant to refuse "help." Under this approach, a staff man can develop a program, perhaps sell it to the top man, and then put it into operation. Line managers will participate whether they think it's effective or not.

The initial program may get started because line managers don't dare refuse to participate, and if it is successful, the situation can change into one of the three that have been previously described. Power and status may become irrelevant and the staff man will be effective because of the acceptance and enthusiasm of line management. But if the initial program is not effective, it will gradually fade away.

Responsibility of top management

Top management also has a responsibility for the training and development of its supervisors. This means that proper philosophy and policies must support the idea that training and development are necessary. Top management should make its position clear by means of a written statement that is communicated to all concerned.

Also, policies should include a tuition refund plan to encourage and support the development of all employees, supervisory and nonsupervisory.

4 Supervisory Decision Making and Employee Participation

Decisions and decision making

A decision is an act of choice. It takes place when one alternative action is selected in preference to all others. On the other hand, decision making is a process, or series of events, leading to a choice and continuing after a choice is made.

Steps in decision making

To illustrate the nature of decisions and decision making, consider the illustration in Figure. Each stage in the process is important if we are to understand supervisory decision making. Therefore. let us briefly examine each phase.

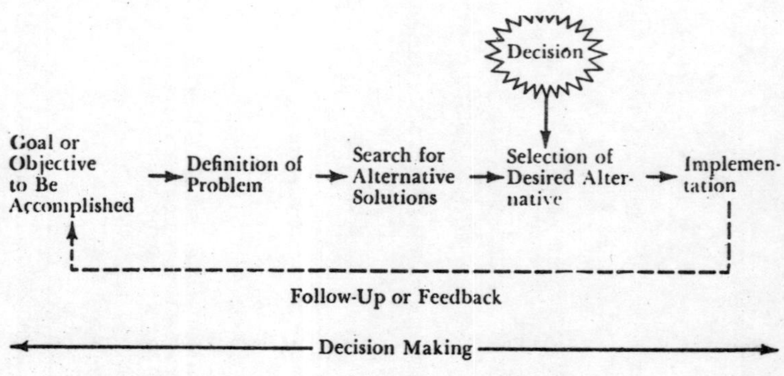

The decision-making process

Establishment of the goal: In making decisions, supervisors are concerned with an objective or a set of goals. This is their standard, their point of reference, when they select among alternative solutions to a problem. The goal may be productive efficiency, work-group satisfaction, industrial peace, or some other end considered desirable and supported by higher management.

Definition of the problem: Before a problem can be solved, it must be accurately defined and analyzed. If, for example, supervisors are concerned about a reduction in the output of their units, care must be taken to analyze the problem thoroughly before taking corrective action. What has changed recently that could cause reductions in performance? Has there been a change in the incentive program? Are there rumors circulating about possible layoffs? Is the union contract up for renewal? These are but a few of the possible questions one might ask.

Search for Alternative: Once the problem has been defined, possible solutions must be generated. It is unusual if only one course of action exists.

Let us assume that we know of rumors about possible layoffs. There are several things that might be done. The supervisor might allow the rumors to go unchecked. In this case, no action is the chosen alternative. Or, he or she may "level" with the group and tell them exactly what the situation is. It might also be advisable to have a member of the personnel department talk to the group. In other words, various alternatives are available to the supervisor.

Selection of the Alternative: After a proper evaluation, the supervisor must decide on the appropriate course of action. This is the point of decision. The choice is made with reference to the goal he is attempting to accomplish. The decision problem is to select the alternative that holds the greatest promise of accomplishing the objective.

Implementation: When the decision is made, the selected course of action must be put into practice. If the group leader decides to hold a meeting of employees to assure them that no plans are being made for layoffs, the conference must be scheduled and the time communicated to the work group.

Follow-up: The supervisor should always be concerned with be coming a better decision maker. Therefore, it is important to monitor the results of a decision. This is a learning process whereby the supervisor reflects on the process and cons of the selected course of action with respect to the goal being sought. Regardless of the outcome, lessons are always learned that can be useful in future decision making.

This, we see that decision making consists of several stages, only one of which constitutes the actual decision. We must recognize, however, that decision making does not stop with the evaluation or follow-up phase. Decisions have lasting effects on the person responsible for their implementation. Perhaps the most common effects are the anxiety and frustration that follow human choices.

When a supervisor chooses one act over others there are always certain aspects of the rejected alternatives that are favorable. Usually, we overcome frustrations by concentrating on the favourable features of rejected alternatives. Although this can be troublesome if taken too far, such reactions are basically functional in a psychological sense because they allow us to continue with some degree of sanity in accomplishing the complex tasks of supervision.

Before looking in greater detail at the problem-solving process, we must examine some different ways of viewing decisions. This is the goal of the following section.

Basic types of decisions

There are numerous ways to look at supervisory decisions. Although we seldom classify them consciously in our minds, some awareness of each can aid in a more successful implementation of the decisions we make.

Means or ends: One of the most effective ways of emphasising the importance of supervisory decisions is to look at the means-ends relationship they are designed to accomplish. This can be explained with the use of the following illustration.

Morgan Parker is a supervisor on the day shift in the Baker Machine Shop. At the present time he is interviewing several applicants referred by the personnel department for a job opening as a machinist's helper. In screening the applicants, Morgan is primarily concerned with hiring the helpful who will be most effective in increasing the performance of the machinist to whom he will be assigned. The performance of the machinist is important to ensure the efficiency of the department. The department's efficiency of the department. The department's efficiency contributes to the overall profitability of the firm.

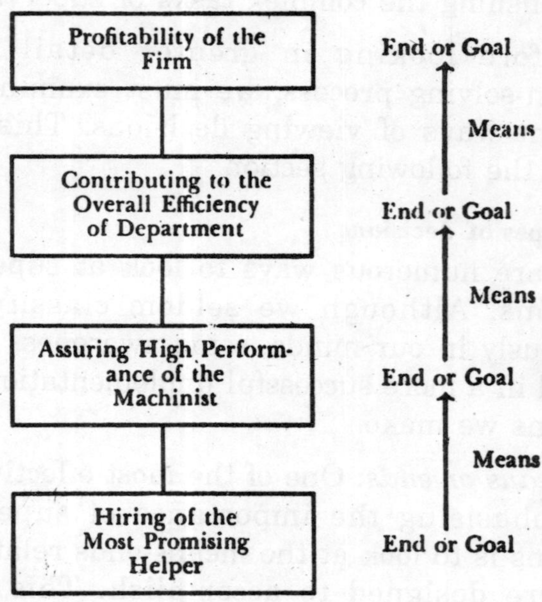

Decisions as means-ends relationships

The logic of the means-ends relationship is important from the perspective of the firm. The selection of the proper helper is the immediate goal. The accomplishment of this goal, however, is the means to a higher level end—the machinist's proficiency. The machinist's proficiency, in turn, is the means to a more efficient department and ultimately to the profitability of the firm.

The view of supervisory decision making emphasis the importance of seemingly routine actions on the accomplishment of organizational goals. In other words, the profitability of a firm, such as the Baker Machine Shop, is dependent on correct supervisory decisions.

Routine and nonroutine decisions: Every supervisory job is a complex mixture of routine and nonroutine decisions. This terminology should not imply that one type is more or less important than the other.

Routine decisions are recurring and predictable. Production scheduling must be done at certain times, and everyone knows it. Schedules can be developed and plans made accordingly. This is also true of shift assignments and released time for vacations.

Nonroutine decisions are not recurring and cannot be easily predicted. Sometimes, without notice, a production line breaks down, an employee becomes ill and must be replaced, or your boss puts you in charge of implementing a new process that has not been used previously. Unlike making a schedule, it is impossible to predict exactly when this type of situation will occur, and when it does, little experience is available to guide you in deciding what to do. The point is simple—we can program, plan for, and anticipate routine decisions. Nonroutine decisions must be dealt with as they develop.

Some outcomes of decision making

To this point we have examined the basic decision-making process and noted that it is essentially a means of systematic problem solving. Unfortunately, the supervisor who carefully follows the process is not guaranteed that successful decisions will always result. To illustrate, consider the following situation.

Lois Dodson is the supervisor of Steno Pool Number Three in the Engineering Department of a large petrochemical firm. In this capacity she is responsible for supervising ten senior typists and for assisting the group in completing the consistently heavy work load. The typists are all highly skilled employees because of the technical nature of work. They are not unionized, but there have been rumors of organizing efforts by the local representative of the office workers' union.

In the past, vacation time has been scheduled on the basis of seniority. If more than one person applies for vacation time around Christmas, for example, the one with the longest service is given priority.

Recently, Lois received vacation requests from Janet Davis and Lawrence Beck for the week of December 25. Only one number of the group can leave on vacation at any given time and both of the applicants have equal time with the company.

Lois knows that Janet Davis' husband is

graduate student at the local university and Christmas is the only time they can travel to visit their families in a distant city. Lawrence Beck, on the other hand, plans to be married on December 23 and wants to combine the vacation with a honeymoon.

Sound familiar? Lois is confronted with a serious, although typical, supervisory decision. Let's see what can result.

First, Loid could decide to allow Lawrence Beck to go on vacation because of some criterion such as the alphabetical order or the applicant's last names. It is also possible that Janet might understand and yield to the decision. In this case a decision has been made and a satisfactory outcome has resulted.

On the other hand, Lois may decide in favor of Mr. Beck and Ms. Davis may be dissatisfied. The obvious charge could be that there is no policy for deciding on vacation time based on the alphabetical order of last names. Here, a decision has been made and conflict has resulted. Both of these possibilities could also be repeated with Ms. Davis going on vacation and Mr. Beck remaining at work.

There are, of course, other possibilities. Lois may decide that since both employees have the same seniority, there is no equitable way of resolving the issue and allow no one to leave during the Christmas week. Or, it may be possible to ask the two employees to come together, discuss the dilemma, and work out a compromise.

Obviously, in a decision of this nature, there is no absolute rule for action. What the supervisor does is a complex mixture of judgment, concern for justice, consideration of group performance, and numerous other factors. The important point is that a relatively routine issue can often become quite complex. Recognizing the complexity of the problem, the supervisor must look at the alternatives and select the one considered most appropriate. At times, reformulating the choices in the form of a decision tree like this can help in itemizing and examining alternatives.

The primary danger is to make complex decisions while assuming they are as simple as they appear. Through a more through and systematic analysis, the supervisor can at least anticipate possible outcomes and prevent, insofar as possible, the anxiety and frustration inherent in decision making. He or she can also prepare, in advance, methods of resolving conflicts that might result.

Decision making: from theory to reality

To this point we have looked at decision making as a precise series of steps one follows in arriving at a desired goal. In reality, this is often impossible.

The supervisor often finds problem-solving situations more confusing than our discussion indicates. For example, problems develop from the very beginning of the process. Often the supervisor is not sure of the goal to be accomplished. Although upper management may devote considerable time to emphasizing the importance of profits, good labor relations, social responsibility, and so on, these objectives are difficult to reformulate into precise guidelines for action. For example, will terminating an unsatisfactory employee increase the efficiency of the department and the profitability of the firm? On the surface the answer would appear to be yes. However, we must ask whether or not it would simultaneously, result in unfavorable labor relations, reduced morale, and lower profits?

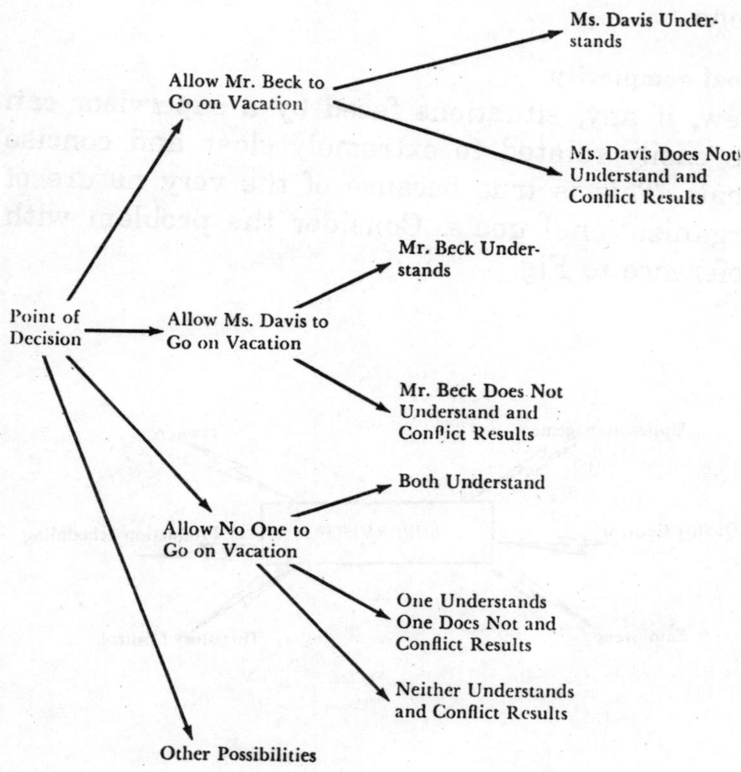

The complexity of supervisory decisions

Another important complication is time. We would all probably agree that systematic problem solving is better than unsystematic behavior. It is also more time consuming. Thus, the practical issue becomes: How much effort can I devote to gathering and analyzing data without using an excessive amount of time? After all, the supervisor's days are far too short already?

The fact is that much of our decision-making behavior recognizes and allows for these complications. We shall briefly look at how this is done.

Goal complexity

Few, if any, situations faced by a supervisor can be easily related to extremely clear and concise goals. This is true because of the very nature of organizational goals. Consider the problem with reference to Fig.

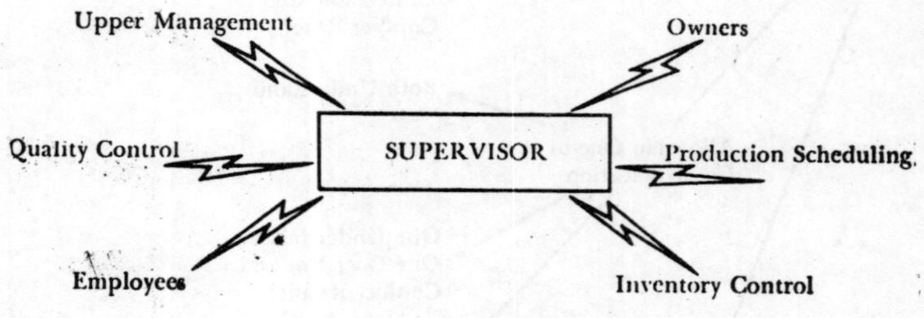

Influences on supervisory decision making

The supervisor here is pictured at the center of a network of relationships. All the individuals in this network are exerting certain influences on the decision maker with regard to their understanding of organizational goals. Upper management and owners are demanding profits, while employees are demanding higher wages. At the same time, production scheduling is insisting on a timetable to ensure that raw materials are available and efficiency utilized. Quality control is concerned with excessive waste, sales is concerned that a sufficient supply finished products is available, and inventory control is upset over rising inventory costs. As a result, the logical means-ends relationship becomes less precise. Not only is it impossible to clearly "picture" the organizational goal, but the relationship among the various organizational interest groups in one of conflict. The efforts of the supervisor are thus directed toward comprising the various interest groups rather than maximising the interests of the owners. This is one reason why supervisory decision makers are often said to *sacrifice*; that is, they try to achieve an outcome satisfactory to all the groups by minimizing conflict. This greatly complicates the maximization of performance. But, there is more to the problem.

Limited knowledge

Supervisors also fail to maximize decisions because of the vast amounts of information necessary in even simple situations. In the case of Lois Lodson mentioned earlier, we itemized some of the options she might exercise, but were quick to admit that other alternatives were possible.

Decision makers generally have limited knowledge for one or more of the following reasons.

1. The problem is too complex to understand, or imagine, all possible courses of action.
2. The objective of some decisions makes complete knowledge unnecessary.
3. The cost and time necessary for gathering all information is prohibitive.
4. Search patterns limit the amount and quality of information generated.

Let us look briefly at each of these.

Problem complexity: There are very few problem situations where we are sure that we know all available courses of action. Even if we should be so lucky, we surely could not know the possible outcomes for each alternative. Yet, knowledge of both these items is necessary if we are to maximize the results of our decision making.

Objective of decision making: Sometimes the task facing supervisors is not to generate alternatives but to analyze and select from among those presented to them. For example, a firm may have a centralized hiring policy where the supervisor reports job openings and the personnel department locates possible candidates. In one case personnel may send three applicants and ask the supervisor to make the final selection. Here, the decision maker may choose may choose any of the three or reject all and ask for more applicants. In earlier event, the supervisor's job is to select among presented alternatives, not to generate new ones. Thus, the objective of decision making is an analysis of alternatives.

Information cost and time: The acquisition of information, or generation of alternatives, consumes time and costs money, neither of which is plentiful in today's organizations. As a result, the supervisor may consciously decide to make a choice after a specific number of alternatives have been generated.

Search patterns: Not all supervisors search for alternatives in the same manner. Some, for example, will generate as many alternatives as possible. Others will make a decision on the basis of only one or a few available options. How supervisors search for information is related to a number of factors such as their personalities, past experiences, time commitments, etc.

Decision making is by its nature an individual activity. At times, however, groups are involved in the process. Probably the most common form of group decision making is the committee, but supervisors may involve others without the formality of a committee structure. Because of this, we must examine the pros and cons of group decision making and the related issue of employee participation.

Group decision making

Supervisors in all types of organizations are frequently faced with the question of whether or not to call on others for assistance in making important decisions. Although we joke about committees and say that no self-respecting supervisor would ever admit that committees are useful, the fact is that most organizations make extensive use of such groups. One survey, for example, found that almost all large firms studied acknowledged the use of committees in decision making. Obviously, groups of this nature are objects of concern to supervisors.

Some oros and cons

If most organizations use committees, they must obviously have some advantages over individuals acting alone. The primary advantages usually include the following:

1. Groups expand the capabilities of individuals. This is particularly true when the groups are structured in certain ways.
2. Group decision making facilities a sense of participation on the part of employees.
3. Representative groups reduce conflict when decisions under consideration have interdepartmental or interunit implications.

Let us look in greater detail at each of the proposed advantages.

Expansion of individual capabilities. All of us have, no doubt, experienced the mental stimulation that can be received from discussing things with others. Often, we think of numerous points that might not have been considered if someone had not made a certain statement.

Although we can be easily stimulated by group numbers with similar backgrounds and experience, we can also increase our creativity by interacting with others who view problems from a different perspective. For example, several foremen of production units may talk over a problem and examine numerous alternatives that would have never been considered by each foreman acting alone. Similarly, if a foreman is placed in a group with supervisors from other areas such as sales, finance, and personnel, more dimensions of the problem are likely to emerge.

Increase participation: Since we will deal with employee participation in the final section of this chapter, only a few comments will be made at this point. For our purposes, we can simply note that when people participate in problem solving they feel more a part of the solution. At least, they feel important because someone has asked their opinion. As a result, implementation of the proposed action should be easier.

Aiding in interunit cooperation: Let us assume that production and sales are experiencing a typical conflict. The production department wants to schedule production runs over the year so as to avoid layoffs. Sales, however, recognizing that orders tend to cluster around certain months, wants production increased during such periods to ensure adequate inventory levels.

It is doubtful that either group would approve a solution dictated by the other. However, by working on a solution through representatives of both groups, they can develop a recommendation more satisfactory to each.

To this point, groups, sound like good things. Lest we be misled, however, we must also note some possible disadvantages. A few of the more important are:

1. Groups are expensive and consume valuable time.
2. Some people are not secure in groups and may be inhibited by dominant personalities.
3. Groups make decisions that are too risky since no single individual is accountable for the outcome.

Expensive and time consuming: Everyone in a supervisory position has probably experienced the frustration of attempting to obtain group agreement on some issue. The presentation and discussion of diverse opinions obviously takes longer than a single person's sitting down and making a choice. Also, it is usually difficult, if not impossible, to schedule a time when all concerned parties can attend meetings without disrupting normal operations.

When the group is assembled, each member's attention is also diverted from primary job duties. The person's pay, however, continues. As a result, group decision making becomes expensive in a monetary sense.

Inhibiting effects on individuals: While a group setting stimulates some people, it frightens others. This can be a special problem where groups are composed of people from different levels of authority. For example, if supervisors and their bosses are members of the same problem-solving group, some supervisors may refrain from making suggestions for fear of their bosses' reaction.

Even where groups are carefully selected to ensure that only individuals of equal organizational status are represented, dominant personalities often emerge. Such people who become very stimulated by group discussions can sometimes discourage less dominant individuals from participating.

Groups assume more risk. Some writers in the area argue that groups consistently make riskier decisions than individuals. The idea behind the argument is that when a group recommends a course of action, no single person is responsible for the outcome. Thus, the group feels more comfortable with risky actions. Research on the subject raises questions about this line of thought, since some studies have shown that groups tend to reach compromises that result in less risky recommendation.

The point of this discussion is that groups offer advantages and disadvantages in the area of decision king. They are useful in building involvement and participation but can be expensive and time consuming. The practical issue for supervisors is that groups can assist in solving problems; however, the issue of participation raises additional points and supervisors should consider in the area of decision making.

Employee participation

Rensis Likert, former director of the Institute for Social Research at the University of Michigan, has worked extensively with the question of "how successful managers manage." On the basis of more than three hundred studies in all types of organizations, he developed a list of six characteristics possessed by good managers. These are:

1. The successful manager is technically competent in his or her job.
2. The successful manager formulates high-performance and challenging goals.
3. The successful manager supports subordinates by showing confidence and trust in them and by listening to what they have to contribute.
4. The successful manager builds effective work groups by involving subordinates in decisions affecting them.
5. The successful manager plans and organizes work so that the group knows what is going on.
6. The successful manager ensures that employees are well-trained.

Three of these items relate directly to encouraging employee participation. Item four specially notes that successful managers involve employees in the decisions that affect them.

The importance of participative management is becoming recognized by national governments as well as individual organizations. For example, in Sweden it is a low that all companies with one hundred or more employees must have worker representatives on their boards of directors. A similar system exists in West Germany.

In this country, companies like Questor Corporation have involved employees in such basic decisions as workflow design with favourable effects on moral and reduced absenteeism. In 1973, the Conference Board completed a survey of 147 organizations in an attempt to determine the extent of employee participation in decision making. Although this survey used certain types of subcategories of organizations, several interesting results were obtained that are relevant for our purposes. First, it noted that more than 60 percent of the responding firms used participative-group methods of problem solving. However, most restricted the participation to middle and upper management levels in the organization. Less than 10 percent involved lower levels of supervision and rank-and-file employees in participative problem solving. Thus, we see an interesting pattern in participative decision making as it exists in reality. It is used, but involvement is limited. Let us examine the topic in greater detail.

Some advantages of participation: Advocates of participative decision making usually base their position on one or more of the following arguments, listed by Tannenbaum and Massarik:

1. Performance can be improved through higher rates of output and increases in the quality of

the work . This is assumed to result from the feeling of greater involvement on the part of employees.

2. Because involvement increases, morale improves. The result is often less absenteeism and lower turnover rates.
3. Better company-union relations develop with a corresponding reduction in the number of grievances filed.
4. There is less resistance to change. Since employees feel a part of what is happening and have been included in decision making, there is less reason for them to resist the implementation of plans.
5. Improved decisions often result because more input has been obtained and a more critical analysis has been conducted.

We see from this list that advocates of employee participation see many desirable effects resulting from the involvement of group members. Production is said to increase, morale is thought to improve, better union-management relations development, individuals become less resistant to change, and better decisions result. If only this were true!

In some cases, no one would dispute the favourable effects resulting from participation. However, there is obviously another side to the coin or no one would be autocratic. Every successful manager would encourage and insist on participation. But this is not the case.

Some disadvantages: All supervisors do not encourage participation because there are certain disadvantages. A few of the more important are:

1. Urgent decisions require fast action. Obtaining inputs from even a few people takes time.

2. Threats to supervisory authority can result from participation. When you ask the opinions of others you have an obligation to consider suggestions seriously. Some supervisors may view this type of inputs as a threat to their position, since they assume that asking the opinions of others is a sign of weakness.

3. The supervisor cannot delegate responsibility. Regardless of how much you involve others in decision making, you alone are responsible for the action taken. Since you are responsible for the action taken, there is less incentive to give up control over decisions to be made.

4. Not all employees want to participate. Some choose not to be supervisors. They do not want to be bothered with decision making and may look upon it as not part of their job.

The choice between autocracy and democracy is not an easy one. For this reason, Le Forest Smith, General director of the YMCA in Orange, New Jersey, suggests that the most effective supervisors are those who can accurately view a situation and decide "when to use group thinking and when to go solo."

5 Principles and Practice of Supervisory Management

Cultural and environmental differences

There are differing opinions on management principles and practice. One view is that management science is similar to all other sciences, which rely on explanations and laws applying universally. Another view is that management science varies depending on the culture and environment applying in each instance.

Research on this latter topic—comparative management—involves analysis of management in different environments and looks at why enterprises show different results in various countries. Certainly investigations show that *management philosophy* tends to vary in different countries but that organisational structuring and growth rely on logical, recognised practices for success.

In this chapter a universal application of management principles and practice is assumed. Features discussed are, first, major principles, the application of managerial skills and the skills cycle. Next, management/supervisor relations are outlined, with particular reference to pressures and demands on managers, the present state of management and how the supervisor should make allowance for managers. Finally, making the best use of time available.

Principles of management

All principles of management may be grouped to fit conveniently into seven main aspects of management activity. These are:

- forecasting
- planning
- organizing
- co-ordinating
- commanding
- controlling
- motivating

Forecasting and planning

These activities involve looking ahead and trying to visualise and plan effectively. Certain principles, now described, should be followed from the beginning to cut down the risks of inaccurate forecasting.

Research

Although the value of constant investigation is recognised and attempts are made to carry it out, in practice it becomes too difficult due to lack of time. People who are under pressure work must make decisions based upon less and less information, with the inevitable consequences. However, the sight of everyone working at high pitch pleases rather than bothers some managers. If managers are overworked it is their own fault for not delegating, but there is a limit if top management restricts staff to smaller numbers than are really adequate. Some managers, too, are unable to assess work content accurately, even after research has been conducted and the information is presented to them.

The following minor principles should be intrinsic to any research:

- *cause and effect* a belief that effects can be traced back to particular causes, which is the motivator when pursuing investigations back to sources
- *comprehension* the results must be measurable and presented in an understandable form to be of practical use in forecasting
- *intelligent observation* studying an activity requires a certain of awareness and appropriate background knowledge for intelligent interpretation to be possible
- *recognition and analysis* following from intelligent observation, the recognition of similarities is essential when analysing the information and knowing how to proceed to the next stage of investigation.

Forecasting

Armed with sufficient information, the individual must now find a place where it is possible to think without undue distraction. Having found the most suitable place, there he or she must marshal thoughts logically and try to visualise or predict future happenings. Some people call this process intelligent guesswork, luck or being psychic.

Forecasting is often done with very little information in difficult circumstances, hence the phrase muddling through. The unknown factor must be taken into account to maintenance. Consider the serious punters who attempt to marshal as many facts as possible on the horses in a race. They take everything into consideration, including factors such as the weather and injuries, which make the results unpredictable with any accuracy, in order to lessen the odds as much as possible.

The principles of good forecasting are:

- use all sources of information
- gain the maximum amount of information possible in the time available
- work in surroundings conducive to thought
- take account of the unknown factor.

Planning

The next is to determine the targets or objectives and plan a way to reach these goals.

All industrial activities must be considered in the light of the available resources so that plans will be realistic. The good planner will be thinking along lines of economy, which implies that his or her designs are simple, standardised and make due allowance for changes and each item is weighted depending on its importance to the plan.

Scientific control is not possible, unless a plan is based upon a timescale. Planning on this broad front means deciding *what* shall be done, *where, when, how* and *by whom*. It involves not only readjustment of objectives as new information flows in, but also revision of policies, programmes, budgets, systems, organisation and controls.

Top management's task is *strategic* planning of overall policies, objectives, finance and control. This is implemented by managers senior supervisors who are responsible for *tactical* planning, or how the objectives are to be achieved in the time given.

Supervisors then plan - on a short-or medium-term basis - the actual achievement of broad plans using the resources available. This is *process* planning, involving scheduling, progressing, controlling and motivating employees.

The fourth and final phase must logically end with the shop floor or office where employees plan their work in order to complete the jobs allocated to them within the established time limits.

Organising and co-ordinating

Organising means arranging for everything to be at the right place, at the right time, so that work may proceed according to the plan. Co-ordinating means ensuring that all the formal activities of the concern are combined to form a balanced, effective organisation.

The phases that lead to co-ordination are:

- *planning* which includes organisation design or establishing the structure

- *staffing*, which is completed under the aspect of command
- *aligning everyone's efforts*, which is the eventual effect of co-ordination

When employees agree to co-operate and naturally participate willingly, management will be able to co-ordinate successfully. An underlying condition is the ability to lead and motivate people. It is pointless, therefore, for management to complain that employees will not co-operate, when the solution is within its own hands to create the right conditions that encourage and promote co-operation.

Co-ordination is achieved if all the activities are arranged and adjusted in time and situation to ensure smooth economic running and progress towards objectives. Smooth economic operation is an all-embracing term that includes the absence of selfish interests, that balancing of units and adherence to plans.

The problem of balance begins with the co-ordination of main activities or functions by the managing director and continues through to the level of the supervisor who co-ordinates the activities of that section or department with other sections. Balance is made possible by allowing unrestricted input of both information and production assemblies from those who supply the section and unrestricted output to the receiving sections in turn. If the chain of movement is broken, production is off balance and the co-ordinating effect ceases. In this sense, co-ordinating is an intentional active principle.

Commanding

Commanding means giving orders and issuing instructions *and* deciding when and how subordinates should carry out the work. Maintaining command includes making decisions about the relative priority of the jobs that need to be done and ensuring that discipline is kept at a reasonable level that is consistent with good working arrangements. Effective leadership is essential for commanding and motivating.

Although organisation and co-ordination are discussed together because all the principles of organisation are used to achieve co-ordination, in practice command must fall between the two for the following reasons. When the design and planning stage is completed, the next step is to appoint competent staff to the positions drawn up in the organisation plan. Upon completion of staffing, when the individuals are assigned to their jobs and given appropriate duties, authority and responsibilities, they will immediately start to issue instructions. Command becomes operational at this point and its effectiveness will depend upon the ability of managers and supervisors to raise morale by fair and just treatment and to lead in the right direction.

The guiding principles for achieving effective command follow.

Alignment of interest

All effort must be directed towards the general interest. Self-interest must take second place, otherwise command has failed.

Staffing

Appointing managers of the right calibre, consistent with company policy.

Morale

The acid test of command is unmistakably the general feeling of all employees - majority and minority groups - towards management and the company. Much ill-feeling and friction is possible between the two sides, so it takes courage and faith to carry out a long-term programme for morale improvement. A permanent change in management's attitude is essential, otherwise relationships will deteriorate rapidly again.

Adequate payments and appropriate penalties

Adequate payments for services and appropriate penalties for mistakes are two essential principles that should be second nature to the competent manager. Fairness and justice are essential to maintaining a good reputation. Any attempt to show favour to one person results in antagonising the rest. Where it is humane to deviate from the rule, the reason must be made known, whenever possible, if the circumstances are not already common knowledge.

Active participation

People must be allowed to expand their capabilities by using their own initiative, criticising and making suggestions openly with no fear of rebuff. In these conditions they feel more important and develop enthusiasm and drive in response to the progressive atmosphere.

Controlling

Checking performance and taking action to remedy deviations from the plan involves a constant vigil on all stages of the work and the costs incurred.

Effective control demands, *first,* full knowledge of the plans and instructions to proceed, *second,* accurate feedback on operations and results, *third,* a common measure to guage the amount of deviation from the plan and, *fourth,* positive action to correct the deviations.

Scientific control is not a haphazard affair; its operation is very demanding and cannot be switched on and off at random.

The board of directors is supplied with control information by the managing director to check on board policy and programmes, generally from the financial viewpoint. Management accountancy techniques and all the financial control systems connected with them provide the machinery for control throughout the company.

On the production side, information about labour, machines, materials, quality and output provides supervisors and specialist with control figures. Similarly, information about sales in cash and quantity and all the distribution expenses provides management with control statistics. All the information prepared must be worthwhile, providing figures at an economic cost for some positive purpose.

Motivating

Each managerial activity is dependent upon all the others, hence the main difficulty of thinking about a particular one in isolation. Managing is a combined operation that demands a wide, balanced, human outlook, tempered by the use of a multitude of principles.

Probably motivation - the inner force that stirs people from lethargic attitudes into dynamic action is the most neglected aspect of management. Half-hearted attempts to improve matters, which are most often abandoned, irritate and depress employees; they naturally fail to respond to fresh encouragement and the blame is nearly always laid unfairly on their heads.

Successful motivation of employees requires a complete change in the outlook of most managers who are either unenthusiastic or too cynical or set in their ways to change. Long-term programmes are needed, even though results are sometimes not seen for a few years, to overcome management's faults and misconceptions.

The strong tie between motivation and co-ordination is apparent when the principles involved are considered. These include:

- job enrichment programmes
- constant communication to everyone of all relevant information concerning the business
- encouragement of participation and self discipline

- ambitious education and training schemes
- joint consultation
- personnel counselling
- fair schemes of pay, work and welfare

a sincere management.

The skills cycle

Underlying and often permeating the principles described above are certain basic management skills that also apply to supervisors. By appropriate training it is possible to improve these skills through he repetitive process of practice and adjustment.The development of each skill also depends upon the degree of education in certain disciplines or knowledge areas.

Naturally there is a tendency for the disciplines to overlap into more than one skill and in actual operation the dividing line between some of the skills becomes blurred. For the sake of clarity, Fig. indicates these skills in sector form to show the cycle effect, which operates in a clockwise sequence, when logical thought is applied to the work process in any situation. The diagram also indicates some ways of checking on the supervisor's performance as he or she develops. A confusing factor is that, during the course of a working day, the supervisor will have to cope with many situations and people, which means that several of these cycles are in operation at any one time.

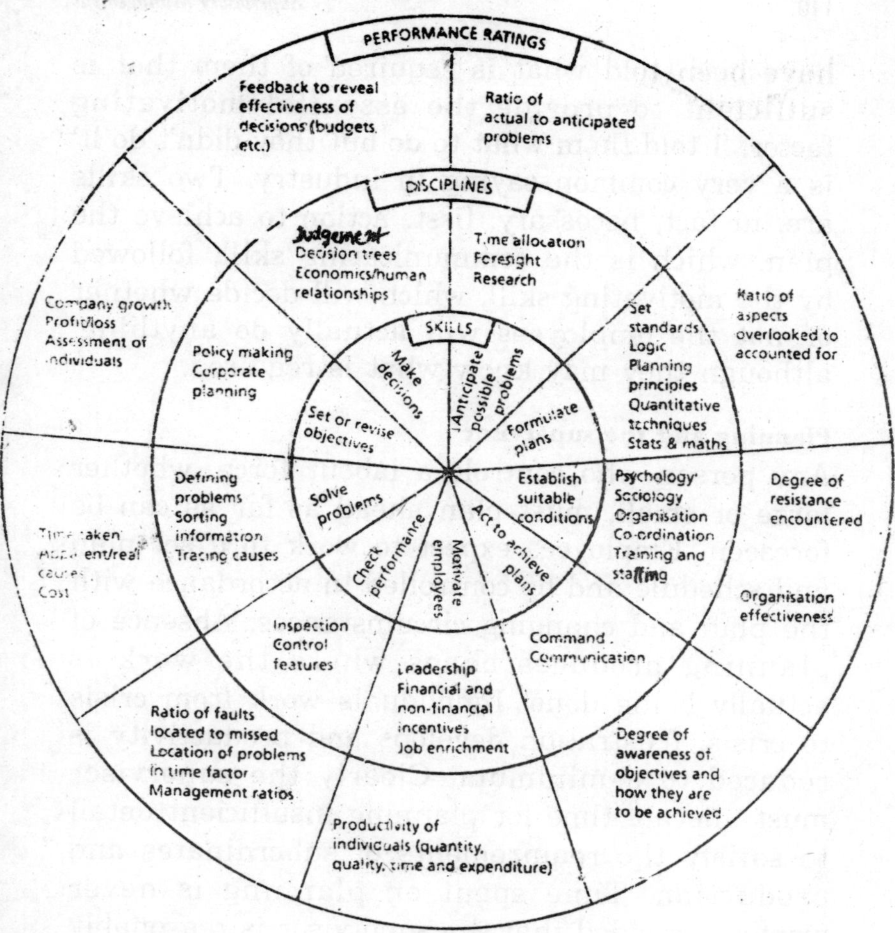

The skills cycle

The diagram can also be used to break down certain principles into component skills. For example, the skills associated with control are to establish suitable standards, to check performance and to make decisions to correct the deviations that occur. A further use is to locate operating faults. For example, the tendency for some supervisors is to think that so long as employees have been told what is required of them that is sufficient to provide the essential motivating factor. 'I told them what to do but they didn't do it' is a very common saying in industry. Two skills are, in fact, necessary: first, action to achieve the plan, which is the communicating skill, followed by the motivating skill, which will decide whether or not the employees will actually do anything, although they may know what is required.

Planning and the supervisor

Any person who controls a labour force, whether large or small, must plan ahead as far as can be foreseen. Employees expect to work to a set plan and schedule and be controlled in accordance with the plan and changing circumstances. Absence of planning produces chaos where the work is actually being done. Individuals work from crisis to crisis, frustration develops and productivity is reduced to a minimum. Clearly the supervisor must allocate time for planning insufficient detail to satisfy the requirements of subordinates and production. Time spent on planning is never wasted, provided that the supervisor is reasonably proficient at the task. The extra thought should result in more accurate and detailed plans, with less risk of having overlooked possible difficulties. There is more likelihood, therefore, that the plan will be successful.

Planning supervisory activities

Most supervisory activities lend themselves to planning which leads to more effective supervision. A cross-section of the main aspects is given below.

Production

A large range of separate plans makes up the overall plan for production. Machine capacity, labour utilisation, scheduling workloads, supplies of materials, provisions for tools and equipment, safety devices, batch quantities and all other resources are planned and combined to form the production plan.

Within this plan, the supervisor's section generally forms only a part of the whole production, which means that co-ordination with other sections is of primary importance. He or she must allow for this factor and be able to accept work in accordance with the overall production, supply work in sequence to the next section and be prepared to help in emergencies.

Objectives

Objectives must be intelligently planned to fit into a timescale within the capabilities of performance. Establishing unrealistic targets is a waste of time. Progress must be controlled and adjustments made as required. The total collapse of efforts to reach specified objectives is bad for morale; therefore, planning with too much optimism should be avoided.

Control

Effective control does not happen by chance. A plan of the particular activity must be drawn up on a time, cost, quality or quantity basis or some other form of standard by which results can be measured. Variances from the plan are now apparent by reference to the data and control is possible by taking appropriate corrective action. Planning and control must always be complementary.

Organisation

Haphazard growth, rigidity and disregard for organisation principles may be avoided with careful planning. Working towards the ideal organisation and making wise changes when the opportunities occur are made easier by conforming to a plan.

Work study

The introduction of work study can be made easier by planning a careful explanation to employees. The programme may include posters, literature, personal letters, films and introductory talks. Work study can be introduced with a minimum of disruption in this manner.

Planning the actual work to be studied may be based upon those sectors that are:

- causing hold-ups
- expensive to operate
- trouble-spots
- relatively high labour turnover areas
- where an increase in output is contemplated.

Communication

Communication may be improved by having experience in running the particular section and by a plan of methods, routes and check systems. Suitable improvements may be planned to eliminate weak spots. A simple plan would begin with an assessment of each communication between supervisor and subordinates, thus revealing its importance, the time factor, the cost and the confidentiality factor. It should then be possible to select the best means of communication for each kind of message from the methods available. The objective is to ensure that the right person receives the right message at the right time and interprets it in the right way.

The daily routine

Planning the way each day is to be spent is important. Certain daily tasks cannot be neglected and, unless the supervisor plans the day or week, the risk of some vital activity being overlooked is greater. Simple check-lists are useful reminders of daily and periodic tasks that otherwise may easily be forgotten. More elaborate activities that extend over long periods may be charted on the wall by using a time base across the top of a sheet and an activity base down the left-hand side to form a grid. Each square may be either ticked or used to enter details if on a larger scale. Pending jobs may be, similarly, progressed or listed, a pending tray or file being used for the paperwork.

In conjunction with delegation, the supervisor should plan to off-load duties as the opportunities occur and use the freed time for more important tasks that have been rather neglected.

Health and safety

Reducing the accident rate and promoting health depend upon detailed planning by management and the supervisor. Planning for safety is an integral part of reducing accidents to a minimum by making machinery and equipment less hazardous and promoting the right attitudes towards safety. The supervisor's social responsibility cannot be fulfilled unless he or she plans to prevent accidents rather than wait for them to happen and *then* reduce the risk.

Maintenance

Planned maintenance is similar in some ways to planned safety. Time and cost may be cut by planning the maintenance of machines to reduce the risk of breakdown. Replacing those components and assemblies whose life is limited before a breakdown occurs ensures smooth output flow.

Training

Training must be treated seriously as a planned activity to improve productivity by introducing better methods and safer ways of working to reduce fatigue and frustration.

Planned training includes induction training schemes, training employees to use new machines as obsolescent models are superseded, training newcomers at weak points where hold-ups are occurring or are likely to occur and making hazardous operations safer by increasing the skill of the employee.

Motivation

All that was said above regarding management and motivation applies at the supervisory level also. All factors that affect motivation closely interact so the approach must be on a broad front so that employees can develop their capabilities and enthusiasm simultaneously. The plan must be long term and sustained in application. New techniques of leadership and supervision, group activity, organisation, human relations and job satisfaction are essentially long-term projects and need a sustained effort whereas financial incentives are short term and often short-lived as motivators.

Human relations

The supervisor who plans successfully also improves relationships with subordinates. They have more faith in a leader who defines objectives, plans carefully and shows command of the situation. Morale will rise as schemes materialise and employees benefit from effective plans.

The above-mentioned topics are only an indication of the many activities that must be planned by the supervisor. Savings in time and nervous energy and possible by planning any activity. Some guides to better planning are now given, together with the characteristics of a sound plan.

Guides to better planning

- *Planning must not be postponed:* Planning is hare work but, without plans, work becomes much harder.
- *Planning must not be selfish:* The part played by the section within the organisation must be

remembered; therefore, co-operative and co-ordinated elements are essential in plans.

- *Always plan within a realistic timescale:* Effective control depends upon measurement of work or a project within a period and, furthermore, employees tend to work within periods related to output, which means they work to time targets.
- *Marshal as much information as possible:* on employees, machines, equipment, materials and other resources. Use up-to-date information and all available resources.
- *Aim to provide as much detail as possible:* There is less chance of overlooking important points and more chance of work proceeding to plan if there is thorough coverage.
- *Ask for opinions and ideas:* Many individuals have something to contribute towards a sound plan; therefore, ask now and avoid adverse criticisms later.
- *Define the problem or objective clearly before planning commences:* Look at the *whole* project and break it down into its constituent parts to ensure full coverage and to provide a workable scheme.
- *A sound, workable and economic plan is the outcome of something more than logical marshalling of information into a set routine:* Certain intangible qualities must be cudgeled into activity within the supervisor's mind. He or she must be imaginative and creative,

exercise judgment and perception and yet retain an objective, critical approach to the problem.

- *Have the courage to stand by the plan.*
- *Check and revise the plan as circumstances change.*

The following are ten characteristics of a sound plan:

- economic, within the financial capabilities of the concern
- workable, considering the resources available
- thorough, allowing for most contingencies
- balanced, to blend with other plans
- resilient, to cope with unforeseen changes
- worthwhile, fulfils a desirable purpose
- attractive, creates interest among all who are concerned
- detailed, to establish adequate procedures
- timely, to obtain maximum benefit
- impersonal, avoids personal prejudices.

SWOT analysis

Useful in planning, problem solving, decision making, case studies and projects, SWOT stands for analysing Strengths, Weaknesses, Opportunities and Threats.

Studying situations or organisations under these headings and completing the information in four boxes forces an analysis of the situation from diverse viewpoints. Thus, a more comprehensive base of knowledge about how the company works provides opportunities to build on the company's strengths, minimise its weaknesses, take advantage of opportunities and allow for external environmental difficulties. The technique applies equally at different organisation levels.

APACS

This practical application of SWOT provides a logical framework for study; the letters stand for Adaptive Planning and Control Sequence. The steps are:

- state objectives
- appraise SWOT
- specify activities involved
- evaluate courses of action
- forecast results of alternative actions
- implement the chosen plan
- assess outcome
- modify accordingly

Problem solving

Problems and choices are met in all supervisory and managerial activities and must be dealt with, reputations being built or ruined on individual performance. The supervisors often automatically establish standards for a vast number of control aspects connected with problem solving without fully realising the implications to their subordinates. Human behaviour is a typical example where the supervisors expect a particular code of conduct in many different situations. They are faced with a problem when a standard is violated and if they fail to investigate, find the cause and make a decision, control is lost.

Often many managers do not even realise that there is a problem to be solved. Unfortunately problems do not solve themselves effectively, although some managers will openly admit that they believe that if a problem is left for a sufficient length of time it will solve itself. Such managers have not bothered to check on the results of this negative approach, which ultimately brands them as ineffectual.

Standards

Employees also apply their own standards to many aspects connected with their job. One operator, for example, may switch off a machine immediately a fault is suspected, whereas another may wait until a more obvious sign appears. This range of standards among individuals becomes important when it comes to problem solving. One operator, for instance, may report that a machine failed to start when switched on, whereas another may state that when the machine was switched on a smell of burning was noticed. Careful definition of the problem in the latter case immediately narrows down the cause of the fault.

The use of standards - in a broad sense - for gathering information should not be ignored. The approach to obtaining the facts as they appear should be made on a basis of comparison to find a common factor or an isolating component within that factor. A line of machines, for instance, may be powered from the same electricity point; if one machine suddenly ceases to run, the fault may be isolated to a particular section if the basis of comparison is applied by stating whether or not the other machines continue to run. Investigating a problem in this way helps to isolate areas quickly where the cause is likely to be found.

The use of standard practice or standard set-ups is common to many facets of industrial activity. Some examples are the following:

- *the use of raw materials in batches* if faulty work appears it may be isolated to a particular batch that is below standard
- *planned maintenance programmes* when a machine develops a fault it may be possible to trace it to the last maintenance job
- *shift work* a mistake may be isolated to a particular shift or time coinciding with the changeover from one shift to another.

To summarise: problems must be actively solved; the art of recognising and carefully defining problems must be developed the causes of faults may be more effectively located by looking for common factors and isolating the unusual aspects within those factors, thus tracking down the trouble by means of a logical step-by-step approach.

Intuition

This apparently simple, rapid method is.essential when coping with common daily problems. The cause is often immediately apparent, thus simple and complex problems may be solved effectively in this manner by the experienced supervisor. The obvious danger lies in not appreciating the *whole* problem because of a lack of experience and knowledge and jumping to conclusions. Automatic problem solving of this nature can also be dangerous when a recurring problem - normally having a standard cause - suddenly occurs through a new cause not foreseen at the time. Nevertheless, fully use of this method is essential considering the time factor.

Using intuition, current experience or *ad hoc* rules of thumb to solve problems is also termed *heuristics*. A heuristic system applies tentative solutions and is subject to alteration as the situation changes. It is therefore useful when problems are vague, which is not unusual.

Analytical thinking

To avoid the dangers of intuitive thinking, logical deduction is often used The approach is to arrive at an indisputable solution by analysing known, factual information. Thus, there must be one, unique answer that is predictable and the assumption is that the problem has only one solution. For example, if 240 working hours were lost in the assembly section last month, 25 per cent of which were due to absenteeism and 10 per cent through sickness, the answer in hours is 60 and 24respectively. However, if the question is how to cut down the high absenteeism rate, there are many answers and imagination is needed, which makes it a *creative problem* requiring creative thinking in its solution.

Creative thinking

If things or ideas that were previously unrelated now *have* to be related to arrive at an answer, the individual must use creative thought. To improve creativity there are various training schemes and techniques that may be applied. A popular method is 'lateral thinking', which was developed by E de Bono.

Group discussion and brainstorming

The use of groups for creative thinking was developed in the Thirties. The techniques generally conform to a number of basic concepts that concentrate on breaking down the inhibiting barriers to creativity. Typical examples are: to suspend judgement on other peoples' ideas; to allow everyone to 'freewheel' so that any ideas - regardless of whether they make sense - are proposed; to produce as many ideas as possible; and to cross-fertilise all the ideas to see if something new emerges. This is called *brainstorming* and is based on the thinking associated with value analysis.

The main barriers to creative thinking are a tendency to think that there is only one answer, to restrict thinking within a narrow self-imposed framework, to give answers that sound reasonable, to allow the obvious statements to go unchallenged and to worry too much about looking a fool. A good group leader will overcome these barriers.

The technique is easily adapted to most problems and, apart from creative thinking, is useful for developing interpersonal relationships.

Lateral thinking

This system is designed to help the mind escape from vertical thinking and move into lateral thinking. By using various techniques associated with challenging preconceptions and rejecting yes/no thinking it is very easy to convert people into a new way of thinking creatively.

The system has achieved world-wide success but it is essential to read E de Bono's book, *Lateral Thinking,* first.

Synectics

This series of techniques in imaginative problem solving is complex and really should be practised with the aid of authorised practitioners. The body of knowledge is considerable as the techniques have been developed over a long period. They include overcoming 'right-brain' thinking and involving sophisticated group behaviour.

Morphological analysis

This form of creativity is based upon the use of a series of dimensions that are examined in relation to each other and to the possible elements within each dimension.

The analysis is complicated and demands a

considerable amount of preparation. A typical example is to use two dimensions, such as products and markets. Elements for each dimension are listed and combinations are established to trigger off ideas.

Logical approach

A logical approach to problem solving may be established in the following way:

- *set standards* establish standards for as many activities as possible - in other words, set your sights
- *measure activities* measure actual results against established standards to highlight deviations
- *assess deviations* a deviation may be favourable or adverse:

  (a) *favourable* this is a situation nevertheless, the cause should be traced and identified for revising standards and increasing effectiveness

  (b) *adverse* this is a problem that is detrimental to the plan so the cause must be located and decisions made.

- *carefully define the problem* a complete, detailed description of the problem is essential
- *investigate* judge the time factor as the supervisor generally has to work to a definite termscale, then search for information and learn to distinguish between facts, inferences and value judgements

- *analyse and establish the cause* draw up a detailed analysis from the information available, look for indications leading to the source and establish the cause, thus solving the problem - successful elimination of the cause or avoiding a recurrence depends upon making a correct decision.

When assessing information, the source and the number of mouths that have passed it on are of prime importance. The reliability of the source and the distortion factor - as information passes from one person to the next - cannot be ignored. The well-known games of Chinese whispers, making up a sentence and passing it round in a group of, say, ten people, often produces bewildering results, bearing no relationship to the original sentence. This can happen, to some extent, in the workplace. The only sure way to be certain that something is a fact is to see it for yourself; unfortunately there is seldom time and it is impracticable in many instances.

A further confusing point is the inability of some people to distinguish between facts, inferences and value judgements. Each one has its usefulness, but the danger lies in mistaking one for another. Here is a typical example of the three: two people decide to walk from A to B along a street that is often very congested with traffic. The lamp-posts are a standard distance apart and, as the two people walk at a set pace, one takes the time between two lamp-posts and calculates their speed as, for example, two and a half mph. This is a *fact*. From the calculated speed a further reckoning indicates that they should arrive at B give minutes earlier than they intended. This is an *inference* because any number of situations may arise that will affect their estimated time of arrival and therefore it is a conclusion or deduction from a given fact. One then says to the other, 'It is quicker to walk along this road these days because the traffic is so congested'. This is a *value judgement* because it is an *opinion* based upon a series of events over a period that have not been accurately measure or analysed.

Decision making

Making decisions involves the consideration of a number of conflicting factors such as the objective, degree of ruthlessness necessary, humane treatment of people, cost and effectiveness. he supervisor's reputation is directly affected by the ability to weigh these standards sensibly. The choice is tempered also by two conflicting groups, his or here superiors and subordinates.

One method of making decisions is to use a logical approach by placing each standard in priority sequence. The natural priority is to establish and reach the objective. Having stated this, the next priority may be the cost. Assessment is mainly intelligent guesswork based upon considering the courses of action and weighing their probable effect on individuals, general effectiveness and the inevitable undesirable results.

Establishing priorities is a personal matter in which good sense is essential. Which decision is made must depend to some extent on morale and the prevailing industrial atmosphere. Ruthless decisions that cause a deterioration in relationships indicate the inadequacy of the supervisor to appreciate hidden costs and the intangible effects of causing frustration.

To complete the cycle of events, new standards must be set to check the effectiveness of the decision, so that variances may be seen and any new problems brought to light for further action.

A logical approach to decision making may therefore be summarised as follows:

- aim to reach the objective
- consider various courses of action
- weigh the factors involved, for example, individuals, cost, undesirable after-effects, morale, etc.
- choose a course of action
- set standards to check after-effects
- follow up and revise if necessary.

Type of decision

Clearly the *type* of decision is an important feature. Low-grade decisions not directly affecting employees, such as cleaning programmes and garden maintenance are acceptable, as are high-grade decisions where specialised knowledge and heavy expenditure are areas for which consultation is pointless. However, high-grade decisions that directly affect employees, such as pay, overtime rates, working methods and automation, obviously need consultation and acceptance, as do low-grade decisions such as holiday arrangements and rest periods.

Discretionary limits

The number of authority levels in the organisation determines the degree of decision making allowed. Typical discretionary limits are easily identified as they will usually be based upon job titles and levels. First, strategic levels include top management to handle policy making and senior management to take structuring decisions. Second, tactical levels include middle managers to make interpretive decisions and supervisors to make situational decisions.

Social aspects

Companies are now expected to make decisions based upon social considerations, but often social issue are vague and only become involved when all aspects are included. Difficulties often arise over interpreting legislation, monopolies and their effects, satisfying all cultural factors and conflicts between what needs to be done for the company's survival and what should be done to provide the best conditions for the workers.

Arguably there could be decisions that would conflict with *shallow* social factors but that are fundamentally sound and would benefit society as a whole. However, excessive appropriations of revenue at the expense of society is obviously suspect and may even warrant state intervention to reduce misuse of such economic power.

Ethical considerations

The supervisor may often be confronted with difficult decisions, conflicting loyalties and cultural conflict when ethics are involved. Ethics are essentially subjective, personal feelings about human behaviour. Everyone behaves within a certain code of morale conduct. Situations arise continually where decisions are tempered by ethical considerations, especially when legality, bribery, theft, loyalty and confidentiality are involved. Such dilemmas cause frustration, stress and often upset relationships within the hierarchy.

Resolving ethical issues depends upon many circumstances, such as acceptable practices in certain countries and companies, the flexibility of individual moral codes, rigid interpretation or adjusting to each case and acting within the best interests of the company, employees, managers or society.

Legal aspects

Bearing in mind the wide range and complexity of legislation, whenever there is doubt, consult a specialist.

There are many general laws affecting supervisory management. These include: contract, tort, company formation, debt collecting, business ownership, consumer protection, credit, agency, fair trading compensation and negligence. Considering the enormous mass of detail and ambiguity, consulting an appropriate textbook is helpful but should not be relied upon if the supervisor is directly involved.

Political aspects

As already indicated briefly, a logical decision-making process may not take into account the external environment and cultural features. Unless explanations, participation at the early planning phased and consultation generally are employed, internal political problems may arise. Although sharing the decision-making process minimises the effects of beliefs, prejudices and attitudes that may upset outcomes, there **are** limits beyond which personal responsibility is weakened.

Locating information

The telephone can be used to provide much information to help with decision making by accessing on-line databases and View data. ODBs are systems that hold computerised information. they are located world-wide and use he international telephone network. Over 3000 ODBs are available at the time of writing and they cover many subjects. Searching is fast and accessing is easy. Host organisations advise on the equipment required to use the ODBs and provide passwords to access the system. Some charge a subscription while others charge on a time basis, the cost being shown on the screen at the end of the session.

Viewdata is another system employing two-way communication. The user needs an acoustic coupler or modem and a microcomputer. Central computers store information that can be accessed through a keyboard. Other systems are available such as Prestel, a public Viewdata system, and

Topic, introduced by the Stock Exchange to give up-to-the-second financial information to subscribers.

Management-supervisor relations

The pressures and heavy responsibilities on managers must be recognised. To appreciate the real situation, the present state of management is now examined, followed by proposals on how to make allowances for managers in the circumstances.

Present state of management

In the UK there are some outstanding managers whose success is known world-wide, but the remaining majority are often accused of being poor managers. According to reports, many are not educated and trained in management, lack drive and initiative and cause more problems than they solve.

Indications of incompetence

In the absence of large-scale surveys, indicators are:

- the poor performance of many companies
- state of the economy
- ignoring outstanding research findings and discoveries that are eventually exploited overseas
- poor individual managerial performance compared with counterparts in other countries
- inability to avoid and resolve disputes successfullv

- never-ending accounts of personal experiences from employees, trade unions and customers, all exploited by the media.

The causes

Some of the reasons given by experts for this state are:

- raw graduates are selected then given no further training
- having the right education impresses
- poor selection procedures are followed
- being the right type who mixes well with existing management is considered sufficient reason for employment
- assuming that an effective functional specialist will make a good manager
- possessing the 'right' social background is overvalued
- selecting a ruthless person who, by devious means, impresses
- nepotism, including friends, is practised
- the practice of promoting people according to age, length of service or seniority
- possessing a particular characteristic that overimpresses
- fear of people with management qualifications
- being overimpressed by graduates from certain universities

- failure to attract high-calibre individuals because industry is generally considered to be a dirty general occupation
- lack of financial and physical support of the management education and training system.

Note that many reasons just mentioned have a self-perpetuating effect on managerial selection.

Adverse pressures

Some argue there are conditions that are outside the control of managers but others say that effective managers should be able to *instigate* change. For such former conditions that are often quoted are:

- trying to cope with employees whose national culture or attitude is non-co-operative
- fighting militant trade unions whose selfish aim is to justify their own existence to members by ignoring the national and local effects of their actions
- relying on inadequate supervisors
- trying to combat situations created by poor governmental actions and policies.

Making allowances for managers

To avoid severe frustration, the supervisor must make allowances for managers. Unfortunately individuals usually expect high standards of performance from their superiors but allow their subordinates some latitude.

Five main approaches that help reduce disastrous management-supervisor relations are:

- *be sympathetic* demonstrate an understanding of problems faced by superiors and the difficulties they encounter solving them
- *be mature* show tolerance in any circumstances - eventually mutual tolerance may emerge as the superior recognises the advantages of this kind of relationship
- *set an example* by maintaining due dignity - expect a negative reaction in any situation where the superior is feeling insecure, fearful, confused or inadequate, be ready for rudeness, off-handtreatment and sarcasm, but try to avoid showing contempt
- *be diplomatic* use your knowledge and point out, tactfully, other ways of dealing with situations and solving problems, ensuring that the superior things your suggestions are his or her own ideas and so avoid time-wasting arguments
- *expect strange treatment* and calculate ways of counteracting it, for example:
- for the compulsive talker who has difficulty listening, try interposing and ask question on the subject *you* wish to discuss; surprise might be the response but a reply is also possible
- when the manager keeps you waiting as a way to demonstrate status, try saying, 'Excuse me please, I'll come back later when you're not so busy'

- for the atmosphere creator who causes a reaction before discussion starts, try withdrawing and telephone or send a memo
- for the snob who intensely dislikes anyone beneath his or her status and ignores you, try avoiding confrontations - you are wasting your time.
- for the intellectual snob who will correct your grammar but miss the message, try a memo.

Time management

Making the best use of precious time is common sense, but, unfortunately, it is all too often uncommon. Time management requires careful planning, control and self-discipline. This straightforward task naturally involves allocating time to avoid having to adopt crisis management and poor performance. Two main features are:

- learn management and organisation principles, supervisory roles, communication techniques and work study.
- use the logical approach detailed below.

Initial check

This involves the following steps:

- *record roles and activities* determine the main tasks and measure the time taken for each one during the working day
- *establish priorities* how important is each activity in terms of its vital nature and how long it takes to complete?

- *list omitted tasks* try to determine the tasks that should have been done but were.neglected through lack of time
- *analyse* rearrange items from the above three points to form a comprehensive structure.

Assessing essential aspects

To do this:

- examine the job specification and update if necessary
- determine your main objectives
- check priorities
- clarify responsibilities
- roughly assess the level of performance
- develop a personal plan

Applying principles and techniques

Apart from the management principles already discussed in this chapter, there are the following important aspects.

Using diaries

Examine the range of diaries available to record information. There are elaborate personal organizers with refills, including a diary, addresses references, a notebook and subject tabs; electronic organisers with many facilities; and simple diaries, which are often adequate. Avoid overcomplicated systems, choose one to suit your needs and choose large formats so you never run out of space.

Avoiding timewasters

Activities that waste time are usually glaring as they irritate. Some examples of good strategies are to:

- try to avoid needless switching from one activity to another, concentrating on completing one task before moving on to the next
- take action immediately when information quantity and quality - is not available to avoid similar problems recurring
- attempt to restrict interruptions by diplomatically establishing periods for discussion with subordinates
- determine quite and busy periods and plan particular tasks accordingly, such as creative work and activities that require concentration
- choose appropriate times to contract others, times when they are able to devote sufficient time to you
- do not rely on memory, write everything down immediately, recording in your notes in the appropriate places later if it is difficult to do so at the time.

Communication aspects

- ensure that communications with subordinates and superiors are clear and understood
- conduct all meetings effectively to avoid unnecessary debate; checking beforehand that they are essential and justify the presence of those who do attend

- always listen attentively and write down important points
- choose times to interrupt carefully and so avoid loss of concentration
- liaise with other sections to check that work is not duplicated
- seek out all sources of information and advice.

Management-supervisor relations

Remember to make allowances, as mentioned in the previous section. Attempt to manage or manipulate the superior, aiming to avoid spending unnecessary amount of time with him or her.

6 Communication for Supervisors

Through the use of language, man has been able to record past history and communicate with the people of other generations. However, communication is not restricted solely to the use of language in its forms of talking, listening, reading, and writing. It also includes body movements, facial expressions, and art forms. Even silence can be a form of communication, for example, when you wish a co-worker "Good morning" and hear no reply. In the following pages, however, we will direct our attention to language as the primary means of communication. In doing so, we will define communication as the *process by which we transfer information, understanding, and feeling from one person to another*.

Today's trend toward increased specialization and its resulting inter-dependencies in all segments of society make good communication imperative. However, unlike the signaling behavior of animals, communication through language and speech is not a natural human activity. It must be learned. In other words, we must be taught how to speak, read, and write. Thus, our learned communication skills can be improved.

We hope that after reading this chapter you will have a greater awareness of the complexity of this seemingly simple task that is often taken for granted. This awareness is especially important among supervisors. Any supervisor is a vital communication link between higher levels of management and workers; and, since over 50 percent of a supervisor's time on the job is spent in some form of communication, the importance of understanding communication activities cannot be overemphasized. In addition, communication is basic to all other managerial functions. For example, planning, organizing, coordinating, motivating, and controlling could not be performed with communication.

Unfortunately, although communication skills can and should be constantly improved, they can never be perfected. To have perfect communication, all persons participating in a particular communication activity would have to derive the same meaning from a particular symbol or word. An easy task you might think - just look up the word in a dictionary. This is much like thinking that you can determine the total size of an iceberg by viewing only the portion that appears above the water. Of course, most of the iceberg lies submerged. Therefore, to determine its size, we must consider the total and not merely that part which is most obvious. This is also the case in communication. Just as the largest part of an iceberg lies below the surface, the largest part of the meaning that we attached to a word lies within us. This meaning is standing, attitudes, and emotions.

Actually, knowing the definition of a word is only one of the requirements for accurate and meaningful communication. In addition, this situation is complicated by the fact that many words have more than one dictionary meaning, with our five hundred most commonly used words having over fourteen thousand definitions. Also, the meanings of word change over time, and new words are constantly being added. Thus, communication is indeed a very complex activity.

A model of the communication process

Many models have been developed to characterize the communication process. Some date back as far as the time of Aristotle, who viewed communication as consisting of the speaker, the speech, and the audience. Aristotle's model is significant because it recognizes the importance of receivers in the communication process. In other words, there is more to effective communication than just saying something. Instead, it involves saying something to people who, like the speaker, have certain viewpoints, educational backgrounds, levels of understanding, emotional outlooks, and past experiences. Needless to say, all of these factors must be considered as they relate to the communication process.

Interestingly, the communication model upon which many subsequent ones have been based was originally designed to increase the efficiency with which electrical signals were transmitted and received. This model was developed for Bell Telephone in the late 1940s and was later adapted to human communication. In addition, many other models of the communication process have been developed. As a result, there are almost as many models of the process as there are authorities on the subject. However, most of the models do have a number of common elements. Let's take a closer look at each of them as shown in Figure.

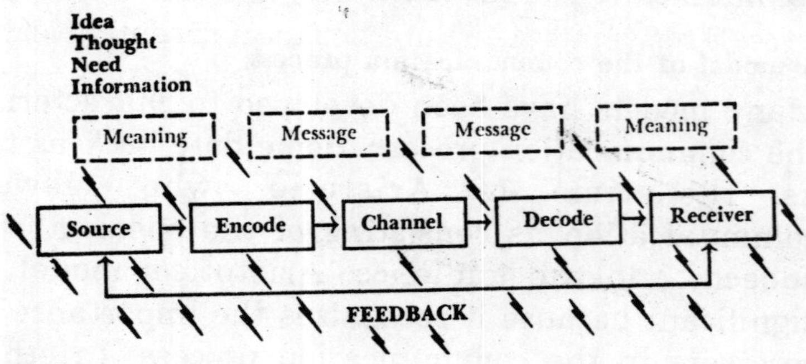

The communication process

Source

Every communication requires an origin or source. The communication activity is initiated because the source wants to respond to the environment in some way. In this sense, all communication can be seen as a response to the way people perceive the various situations in which they find themselves. This is true regardless of whether they are making conversation, talking to the boss, or discussing the day's activities with their families at dinner. For example, suppose a guest is at a party in a friend's home and begins to find the room unusually warm. As the situation becomes increasingly uncomfortable, the guest seeks some way to convey an internal response to the environment. Thus, we have the initiation of a communication event.

The process of human communication involves the transfer of meaning through the encoding of a message by a source who sends it through a channel to a receiver. The receiver decodes the message and provides feedback for the original source. The small lightning bolts represent noise, which is present at all stages of the communication process.

Encode

In all communication, the source must engage in encoding activities. Encoding occurs when the idea to be transmitted is transformed into a set of symbols by the source. In this process, the most commonly used symbols are words. However, we often search for other ways to symbolically convey the idea, information, need, or thought that initiates communication. In any event, we would not be able to formulate and send a message without the encoding process.

Let's continue with our previous example to demonstrate encoding activities. In response to the increasing unpleasantness of the warm room, our party guest searches for some way to let others know he is hot.

Message

A message is the end result of encoding activities. It expresses the purpose of the source, and can include gestures, facial expressions, spoken or written words, or drawings. Since most messages follow a predetermined structure or code, our language can be viewed as a code that determines the grammatical arrangement of words in relation to one another.

In encoding we also search for symbols that will convey meaning, since it is important that our messages be understood. If a message is not clear, the probability of a communication malfunction is high.

The message that the uncomfortably warm party guest transmits to the host could be. "I find it very warm in here."

Channel

The channel is the medium used to transit a message. With most messages, the channels used are those of sight and sound. Any of the five senses, however, can serve as channels for transporting a message from the source to a receiver. For example, a pat on the back given by a supervisor can be used to recognize a subordinate for a job well done.

In the case of our party guest, the primary channel used was that of sound. The guest spoke and the host heard the message that was sent.

Receiver-decode-meaning

The process of communication functions properly

when the receiver decodes the message and derives a meaning from it that is approximately the same as that transmitted by the source. Basically, decoding can be viewed as encoding in reverse, since receivers derive some meaning from the stimulus of the air waves or light waves that have carried the message to them.

As mentioned earlier, it is not sufficient for the receiver to decode a message by merely attaching some meaning to it. Successful communication occurs when the meaning that the receiver derives from a message is similar to that intended by the source. This point cannot be over emphasized, because a failure to understand the intended meaning of a message is probably the greatest source of problems in the communication process.

The root of much misunderstanding lies in the fact that most sources and receivers have differing backgrounds, experiences, viewpoints, knowledge, and emotional make-ups. In turn, these factors determine the meanings we give to certain symbols. Of course, these factors can never be exactly alike for any two people, and therefore, *no two people will ever attach the same meaning to a particular set of symbols.* However, the greater the similarities among these factors, the greater the probability of successful communication.

Getting back to our example, the message, "I find it very warm in here," may be decoded by the party's host to mean that the guest:

1. Has had too much to drink;

2. Has too many heavy clothes on;
3. Finds the room temperature to be high and would like the air-conditioning turned on;
4. Has come down with a fever;
5. Has been engaged in a heated debate about politics with another guest; or,
6. Has some entirely different meaning to convey.

Feedback

How does the source know whether or not the message has been received and decoded correctly? The answer can be found in feedback, another important element of the communication process.

Feedback usually occurs in the form of a response from the receiver. When providing feedback, the receiver encodes and sends a message through some channel to the original source, who is now a receiver. In this way, the original source can tell whether or not the message got through to the receiver. If feedback indicates that the receiver understood the meaning of the message, further communication can take place. If the message was not clear, the source may have to alter the encoding of the message until feedback indicates that the receiver has understood the intended meaning

Feedback does not always take the form, of spoken or written words, however, In a college classroom, for example, a sea of puzzled faces during a lecture should serve as feedback to let the professor know that the message is not getting across.

In our party example, the host's reaction or response to the message, "I find it very warm in here," will let the guest know whether or not the intended meaning was decoded.Let's suppose that the guest did find the room to be too warm and wanted the air-conditioning turned on. If the host says, "I'll turn on the air-conditioning," this acts as feedback to let the guest know that the host derived a similar meaning from the message. On the other hand, if the host's response ie, "what's the matter? Is politics getting too hot for you to handle?" the feedback tells the guest that the host did not derive the intended meaning from the message.

Noise

Noise is anything that reduces the accuracy or fidelity of a communication. Thus, it contributes to miscommunication. By being aware of how noise affects the fidelity of communication, we can take steps to reduce it and hereby improve the accuracy of our efforts in this area.

Noise can be present in all of the other elements of the communication process. At the origin of the communication process, noise occurs when the source perceives an object or activity incorrectly. Noise exists in the encoding stage if the symbols chosen do not properly convey the source's mental perception. Here, the ability to reduce noise depends on the source's mental ability and knowledge of language. The greater these two factors, are, the lower the noise factor will be.

If the form or code of the message is not understandable to the receiver, noise also exists. This can occur when the sender and receiver speak different languages. In such situations, the noise is so great as to make verbal or written communication impossible without the aid of an interpreter.

In the channel, noise can operate to stop the message from getting through accurately. It is difficult to talk to someone when air hammers are operating in the area, for example, And finally, noise is present if the receiver decodes the message incorrectly.

Continuing with our example of the party guest, if he was too warm and wanted the air-conditioning turned on, he might have chosen the wrong symbols to encode his mental perception. If the party was crowded, the conversations and laughter of the other guests could have prevented the message from being heard clearly by the host. In short, the possibilities for miscommunication are endless. Thus, we should constantly strive to improve ourselves in this important area.

Formal communication networks in organisations

In addition to showing lines of authority and accountability, it also serves as a diagram of the organisation's formal communication network. Through it flows the "lifeblood" of the organisation.

Most communication in any organization is either written or oral. Written communication serves as a permanent record that can be referred to again and again. As such, it is usually preferred over oral communication when messages are lengthy or difficult to understand. Common examples of written communication include company policies, rules, reports, memos, manuals, job specifications, bulletins, and contracts.

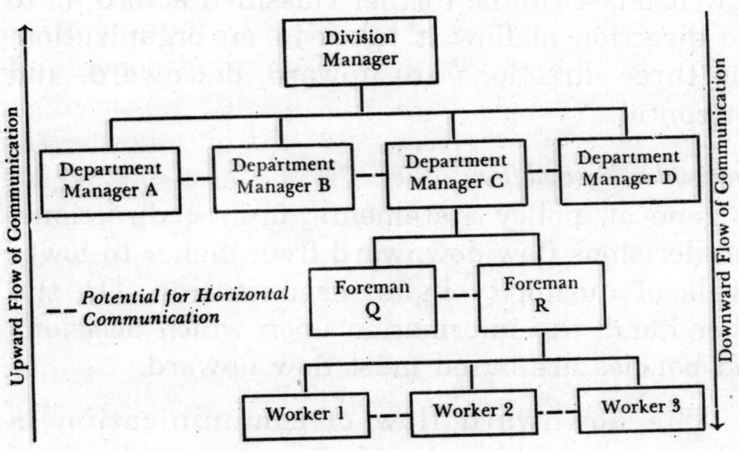

The structure of an organisation as depicted in its organisation chart determines the formal channels of communication

Oral communication usually occurs on a face-to-face basis. The major exceptions to this include telephone conversations, intercoms, and public address systems. Regardless of how oral communication is accomplished, however, its directness is unsurpassed. In addition, feedback is immediate and the sender's tone of voice, facial expressions, and personality can be easily perceived. At the same time, the sender can quickly gauge the receiver's level of understanding. Although these factors serve to improve understanding, oral communication has the disadvantage of being subject to perceptual differences. Thus, misunderstandings that are difficult to overcome often result from our attempts to recall oral messages.

Regardless of whether communication is oral or written, it can be further classified according to the direction of flow it takes in an organization. The three directions are upward, downward, and horizontal.

Downward and upward flow

In general, policy statements, orders, directions, and decisions flow downward from higher to lower levels of authority in an organization. On the other hand, the information upon which decisions and policies are based must flow upward.

The downward flow of communication is rather easily achieved and composes the bulk of all formal organizational communication. However, because downward communication flows naturally from higher to lower levels of authority, it is often overlooked as a potential source of trouble. Just because two people go through the motions of communicating does not mean that they have actually done so. Thus special care should be taken to ensure that instructions, orders, directions, and other types of downward communication are actually understood by subordinates.

Encouraging upward communication is relatively more difficult than is the case with downward communication. In part, this stems from the fact that upward communication runs contrary to the usual higher-to-lower flow of authority found in most organizations. Yet, it is important that supervisors encourage upward communication since, as was previously stated, the information needed to make decisions and formulate policy must flow upward, In addition, upward communication provides a control function and enables supervisors to judge how accurately their downward communications have been transmitted and carried out.

The surest way to choke the necessary flow of upward communication is to encourage it and then to use its contents against subordinates. Perhaps the fear that the content of upward communication will be used against them is the reason why many subordinates have acquired the habit of emphazising only those things that make them look good. Information that does not convey a rosy picture may be suppressed or distorted. For example, a subordinate's pay rise may depend in part upon the judgement of the supervisor. In an effort to make themselves look good, employees may tend to communicate only those things that will favourably impress the supervisor. However, the success of any organization depends on communication that provides an accurate picture of all aspects of its operation, not just the favourable ones. Therefore, the responsibility for encouraging accurate upward communication cannot be overlooked.

Horizontal flow

Horizontal communication takes place between organizational equals, That is, if flows between individuals who are on approximately the same level of authority in an organization. The primary function of horizontal communication is to facilitate the solution of problems arising from a division of labor and specialization. For example, the head of an engineering department and the head of a fabricating department may find that the only way for a production schedule to be met is through a closer coordination of design and fabrication efforts. One way to achieve this coordination lies in the use of horizontal communication flows. Figure 9-3 summarizes this and the other major communication flows.

The grapevine

The upward, downward, and horizontal flows of the formal communication network are only part of the total communication picture in organizations. To complete this picture, the communication network of the informal organization must be added.

Informal organizations can be refereed to as "shadow" organizations. They exist in every formal organization, but cannot be identified simply by looking at authority relationships on the formal organization chart. This is because informal organizations are composed of all the friendship, occupational, and special-interest groups within an organization. The communication network linking members of informal organizations is known as the grapevine. It carries far more information than the formal communication network, and is often more effective.

One of the major characteristics of the grapevine is its speed in transmitting information. In part, this speed is made possible by the fact that the grapevine does not follow the stated authority relationships shown on an organizational chart. Rather, it follows what has come to be known as a "cluster pattern," where information is passed on to a number of other persons, not just one. These persons, in turn, tell a cluster of others and the process continues until the news value of the information declines.

The grapevine can be beneficial as well as detrimental to the performance of the formal organization. Whether the effects are positive or negative depends to a great extent upon the influence that supervisors can exert on informal channels. To turn the grapevine into a constructive tool, one must integrate the interests of informal group members with those of the formal organization. In addition, two other important facts must be considered.

First, the grapevine ultimately develops in any type of organization and is a normal outgrowth of social interaction at all levels of authority. All employees want to know what is going on and how they will be affected. Moreover, they want to know this information as soon as it becomes news. Unfortunately, formal communication systems tend to circulate information rather slowly. Therefore, the grapevine is used to supplement formal communication channels.

Next, it is important to recognize that the grapevine cannot be eliminated. Of course , many supervisors wish that they could do away with the grapevine, and believe it to have only negative effects on workers' attitudes. In part, this feeling probably results from a tendency to equate the grapevine with rumor; however, the two are not the same. Rumors can be described as false informal communication. They arise when people feel that they will be affected by matters over which they have little or no control. Their subject matter can cover such topics as wages, hours, working conditions, supervisory relationships, job security, benefits, and layoffs, to name only a few. Fortunately, rumors represent only a small percentage of the communication carried by the informal network. In fact, most of grapevine information is surprisingly accurate. However, since rumors are misrepresentations and can prove harmful, they should be dealt with as soon as possible.

One way to reduce the occurrence of rumors is to create situations in which people feel relatively secure. This is generally accomplished by keeping formal communication channels open and by transmitting current information. After rumors have started, a supply of facts given to active grapevine communicators in a face-to-face setting is effective in curbing or stopping their spread. These facts should be supplied without specific reference to the rumors, and the person who provides them should have a communication record that is trustworthy.

In summary, it is evident that rumors can have a negative impact on employees' behavior. However, the smart supervisor can use rumors in a positive way to gain additional insights into employees' gripes and misconceptions. Thus, try to determine why and where rumors have started. Then, take steps to prevent similar situations from arising in the future.

Communication barriers

As mentioned earlier, the accuracy of communication can be improved through a working knowledge of the communication process. In this regard, your communication can be made more effective through an understanding of some of the more important barriers to communication. In general, these barriers act to prevent your communication from conveying a complete or true picture. They include perceptual, abstractional, inferential, and symbolic barriers.

Perceptual barriers

The world in which we live is constantly changing. An ancient philosopher demonstrated the dynamic nature of the real world when he stated that a person could never step in the same river twice; the person would be different and so would the river. Thus, reality consists of events and processes, not static things. Unfortunately, because of the limitations of our senses, we are unable to perceive all of our constantly changing process world. However, we are able to observe objects that are the perceptible parts of the events in a process. For example, the book you are reading is constantly moving and changing at this very moment. So are you for that matter, as well as everything around you. Thus, we live in a world of constant motion.

More specifically, to view an object as static when it is constantly changing is an incorrect perception that can lead to inaccurate communication. For example, suppose you are asked about the work habits of Joe Smith, a man you worked with five yeas ago, but have not seen since that time. As you remember, Smith seemed to be lazy and irresponsible. He often came to work a few minutes late and started putting away hit tools a few minutes earlier than anyone else in the afternoon. In short, he didn't carry his share of the work load.

Unknown to you, however, Smith has become more responsible in the last five years and is now considered to be a reliable worker. If you had replied to the inquiry about Joe Smith by saying that he was lazy and irresponsible, you communication would have been incorrect. It would not have reflected the reality of the situation, since it would not have described Smith's true characteristics. Thus, a more accurate way to answer an inquiry of this type would be to preface your remarks with, "When I knew him five years ago ... He may have changed his ways, however. To be sure, why don't you check with someone who has had recent contact with him?"

Abstractional barriers

Abstraction involves focusing on certain details while leaving out others and occurs anytime we perceive a person, an object, or a symbol. In fact, our constantly changing world and the limitations of our sensory organs cause abstraction to be necessary, since we are able to perceive only a small part of what is actually occurring around us.

Abstraction has both advantages and disadvantages that center on the fact that the process permits classification. On the plus side, classifications are valuable in communication because they permit a great deal of information to be transmitted quickly. In addition, the process of abstraction can be extended to an infinite number of classification levels. A classic example of this is provided by the "abstraction ladder" illustrated. Bessie, the cow, is classified on several levels of an abstraction ladder. The cow, Bessie, is uniquely herself and differs from all other objects in the same classification. Because of this quality of uniqueness, any person or object included in a particular classification level will differ from all others. Therefore, accurate communication requires that they not be treated as similar in all respects.

The primary disadvantage of abstraction is that some communication about reality is not the same as reality itself. Problems arise when we confuse the levels of abstraction. As demonstrated by the Bessie example, the more abstract we get, the farther we get from reality. The further we get from reality, the greater the chances of inaccuracies in communication. This is because abstraction leaves out certain details and characteristics at each level. One way of remedying this situation is to use more words at the bottom of the abstraction ladder. Go directly to the thing or object being discussed. Give concrete examples and illustrations. Express the same thought in more than one way. Again, a very simple way to determine whether or not a listener understands your words is to ask. In other words, seek feedback.

Inferential barriers

Suppose we have seen the boss, Mr. Smith, leave the office every afternoon for the past week with his attractive secretary, Mr. Jones. As they get into his car again this afternoon, we may think to ourselves, "If only Mrs. Smith knew what was going on between her husband and Ms. Jones!" However, a closer examination of this situation may reveal that we have no evidence to indicate that anything is going on. We only know that Mr. Smith and Ms. Jones have left the office together every afternoon for the last week and have driven away in his car. Anything beyond these observed facts is inference. Thus, we label as inference anything that we do not know to be factual. As such, inference is an additional form of abstraction. There is nothing wrong with making inferences and we do so many times each day. However, inference become communication barriers when we treat them as facts and, thus, forget that there is some probability that they are incorrect. In our previous example, Ms. Jones may have wrecked her car and Mr. Smith is merely giving her a ride home until she can get a new one. Or, perhaps they are carpooling to save on gasoline. In any event, we must realize that inferences can be incorrect before we can hope to improve the effectiveness of our communication.

Symbolic barriers

The last of the communication barriers to be discussed focuses on words an symbols. Words are not the same as the objects, persons, or events that they represent. In fact, as explained in the section on abstraction, words are several levels removed from the reality which they seek to represent. They are only symbols that represent our mental perceptions and have no meaning in themselves. Thus, the meanings attached to a particular word will vary because of differences in perception, When significant differences in meaning exist, a barrier to communication arises. Thus, try to determine whether your communication has a similar meaning for both you and the receiver. Again, feedback is helpful here.

Improving organizational communication

Probably the biggest and most important step in improving organizational communication is an awareness of the complexity of the communication process. It is not an activity to be taken for granted and, as the basis for all organized activity, it must be performed as accurately as possible.

Greater accuracy in communication can be gained through a knowledge of the workings of the communication process. By being aware of how barriers can enter the process, we can take steps to minimize them. Perceptual, abstractional, inferential, and symbolic barriers demonstrate that we can never communicate reality as it actually exists. However, with an understanding of these barriers, we can work to use those symbols which give the best description of reality as we perceive it.

Finally, being a good communicator involves more than just sending messages. As has been discussed, it also means receiving them. "The Commandments for Good Listening" which follow are practical guides for developing better listening habits.

1. *Stop talking.* You cannot listen if you are talking.
2. *Put speakers at ease.* Help them feel that they are free to talk.
3. *Show speakers that you want to listen.* Look and act interested. Do not read your mail while they talk. Listen to understand, rather than to oppose.
4. *Remove distractions.* Don't doodle, tap, or shuffle papers. It might be quieter if you would shut the door.
5. *Empathize with speakers.* Try to put yourself in their place so that you can see their point of view.
6. *Be patient.* Allow plenty of time. Do not interrupt. Don't start for the door or walk away.

7. *Hold your temper.* An angry person gets the wrong meaning from words.

8. *Go easy on argument and criticism, which will put speakers on the defensive.* They may clam up or get angry. Don't argue; even if you win, you lose.

9. *Ask questions.* This encourages others and shows you are listening. It helps to develop points further.

10. *Stop talking.* This is first and last, because all other commandments depend on it. You just cannot do a good listening job while you are talking.

Summary

Communication is the process by which we transfer information, understanding, and feeling from one person to another. It is the basis for all organized activity. Communication, however, is not a natural human activity. It must be learned. The importance of this fact is that we can improve our communication skills.

Many models have been developed to characterize the communication process. These models have a number of common elements, which include source, encoding, message, channel decoding, receiver, meaning, feedback, and noise. Each of these elements can contribute to communication breakdowns, but decoding activities provide numerous opportunities for barriers to arise. Therefore, feedback is vital in judging whether or not successful communication has taken place.

The formal communication network in organizations can include downward, upward, or horizontal flows. In general, objectives policies, directions, and decisions flow downward through the hierarchy of authority. However, the information upon which these things are based must flow upward, while horizontal communication facilitates the solution of problems arising from a division of labor.

The communication network of the informal organization is known as the grapevine. It supplements the formal network. The occurrence of rumor in the grapevine can be minimized by creating situations where people feel more secure and, therefore, more willing to trust the communication flowing formal channels.

Communication barriers demonstrate how our communication efforts are impeded. Some barriers are created by an individual's perceptual ability, or lack of it. Other barriers are caused by abstraction, in which we focus on certain details while leaving out others. Finally, words and inferences lead to other communication barriers.

Unfortunately, no set of formulas can be given to increase the effectiveness of organizational communication. The process is much too complex. However, communication can be improved through a greater understanding of the communication process and the difficulties inherent in it. We hope that this chapter has contributed to your understanding of these factors.

7 What Every Supervisor Should Know

If you stop to think about it, most of our lives are spent working with and in organizations such as families, clubs, churches, schools, governments, and of course business organizations where we earn our living. We work with all these organizations for only two reasons: we can accomplish objectives through them that we could not accomplish as easily or as effectively by ourselves, and we can do things that we could never do alone.

Some people complain about organization by saying that business would be a good place to work if it weren't for the organization. But think for a moment about the trouble you would have trying to provide food, clothing, and shelter for yourself and your family if you could not work in an organized way with other people. Of course, you might be able to survive, but what you could provide for yourself would not nearly what we have today, and you would have to work as it every minute of the day—not just 40 hours a week. Through organized endeavor, we put a man on the moon. Through organized endeavor, we built a Golden Gate Bridge. For the reasons, we organize ourselves in business—to make the work easier and more effective and to do things that we could not do alone.

What is organization?

Organization is the process of coordinating the efforts of men to achieve objectives in the most efficient manner possible. For our businesses, this means that organizing consists of combining and coordinating what employees do in such a way that they get the most output for the least effort. Thus, in our businesses when we organize ourselves, we are working most effectively toward a goal we want to reach.

What is a line organization?

A line organization is the oldest and simplest type of organization. It's the kind of organization you would find in a small manufacturing plant. This organization is easy to understand, there is no problem about who is your boss, and decisions can be made quickly. Its drawbacks are: if the leader leaves or dies, usually no one is prepared to move in, and the business suffers; and, because the leader has no assistants, he is frequently overworked and places undue reliance on his subordinates. In many cases, this results in jobs being poorly done.

What is a line and staff organization?

A line and staff organization is essentially a line organization to which staff assistants have been added. If our small manufacturing plant's business grew, the owner might need to add accountants to keep his books, a personnel supervisor to look after his employees, a production control man, and an industrial engineer.

The line organization is indicated by heavy lines and is much the same as it was except that more men have been added. The staff organization, however, is new. The owner has hired the staff people to give expert advice and help to himself as well as to his supervisors.

By adding the staff, however, the problem usually arises of how much authority these staff men should have over the shop foremen. For example, does the foreman control the work of his employee or does production control tell the employee what to do? Out of this confusion might come frictions, jealousies, and misunderstandings. This confusion as to who has authority is staff's major drawback. But despite this, the line and staff is the most commonly found type of organization in our economy.

What's the difference between line and staff?

The line organization *directly* aids in accomplishing the goals of the firm. The staff aids *indirectly*. Staff is usually advisory in nature, helping other people know what should be done and how to do it. Staff has no command authority over the line; it only recommends. The staff's purpose is to be on tap for advice but on top authoritatively.

Production and sales departments are most commonly thought of as line organizations, while such activities as engineering, accounting, personnel, and maintenance are usually thought of as staff activities.

Does staff have more authority than line?

It might look as if staff members have more authority, but they actually don't. Remember the staff's job is to advise and help but not to command. The line is the one who has the authority to act and to command. The line supervisor runs his department, not the staff.

If this is true, then how does the staff get away with telling the line what to do? In two ways.

1. If you listen carefully, the staff isn't giving commands to the line. Instead they are saying "This is what I think you should do." or "You'd better do this if you want to improve the quality of your work."
2. When the staff gives this advice, most supervisors take it and make the changes. The supervisor could refuse to do what the staff man suggests, but must of the time the staff man is an expert in his field, and the supervisor knowing this doesn't argue with him. When you go to a doctor and he says you need to have your appendix out, do you argue with him? You could if you wanted to. In fact, you could even refuse to have you appendix removed. You would, of course, have to suffer

the consequences. In like manner, the supervisor can fail to follow the advice of the staff, but in doing so he way have to suffer the consequences.

Are authority and responsibility alike?

Authority is the right to command or act and is the power you have over others. If you have authority, you can cause a person to do something that you want done. Every supervisor is vested with the authority necessary to secure the cooperation of his employees. He might get this cooperation through his dynamic leadership, through coercion and persuasion, or by promise of some economic gain or loss.

Authority is the right to command or act ad is the power you have over others. If you have authority, you can cause a person to do something that you want done. Every supervisor is vested with the authority necessary to secure the cooperation of his employees. He might get this cooperation through his dynamic leadership, through coercion and persuasion, or by promise of some economic gain or loss.

Responsibility, on the other hand, is the obligation that an employee has to his boss to do a job or task that has been assigned to him. The key idea here is one of *obligation*. You are hired to do a certain job; therefore, you have an obligation or responsibility to your boss to do the job he hired you to do.

It wouldn't be fair to hold a person responsible for doing a job without first giving him the authority necessary to get it done. Thus, while authority and responsibility are different, they should go together. Where you have authority delegated, it should be coupled with responsibility.

Where does authority come from?

There are two ideas about this. The first idea or *classical theory* says that authority is delegated from above. If you have authority to hire and fire, you were given this authority by your boss. Suppose you were delegated the authority by him to hire no more than 30 men. You could hire any number up to 30, but you couldn't exceed 30 without additional authority from him. Thus, you get you authority from your boss. He gets his from his boss. And so on up the line.

The other theory of authority is called the *acceptance theory*. The idea here is that the authority you have over your employees is only the authority that your employees give you. In other words, they give you the authority to tell them what to do. In similar fashion, the only authority you boss has over you is what you give him, and the only authority that teachers have over students is the authority that students give the teachers. Suppose you tell your employees that starting tomorrow, everyone must wear red uniforms and yellow shoes to work. Will they do it? If you have authority over them, they will. But they probably won't come to work with red uniforms and yellow shoes—which means you don't have authority over them. Suppose a teacher assigns 115 math problems as homework. Does he have the authority to make you do it? Not unless you give him the authority. Of course your boss or teacher can withhold pay or grades if you don't do what he says, but he can't make you do it unless your give him the authority to command you to do so.

There's some truth in both of these theories. The authority to hire employees comes from your boss—not from your employees. But the authority to force an employee to do a job a certain way comes from the employee and not from your boss. Thus, part of every supervisor's authority, the right to command, comes from his boss and part comes from his employees.

Why is delegation of authority important?

It's the key to organization. If you don't delegate, you won't have any organization—only one-man operations. No one expects a supervisor to personally tell every employee what to do, or to inspect every product, or to prepare shipping papers on everything that goes out. But he may well be responsible for seeing that all this is done, and the only way he can get it done is to delegate authority to his employees. Since the job of a supervisor is to see that his department operates smoothly through the efforts of his employees, he must, therefore, delegate authority to the appropriate employees in order to get the work done.

Another point to remember is that authority should only be delegated to a person who has both the knowledge and the competence to make a decision. If he has information about the job but is not competent to make a decision, he should not be given authority to make the decision. Likewise, if he has competence to make the decision but does not have sufficient information, he should not be delegated authorities and required to make the decision. If you delegate authority to a person who does not have both competence and knowledge, you will probably get bum decisions.

How should you delegate authority?

1. Call in the employee to whom you are delegating the authority, and tell him what authority you are delegating to him. Give him the whole picture and scope of the job. Tell him clearly what he has to do, how far he can go, and how much you will check on him. Tell him the relative importance of the job and how it fits into the scheme of work. Remember that you understand the total situation, that you can see the whole picture, but that an employee does not have your vantage point. When he comes to a crossroads and has to make a decision, you want him to choose the right road, but unless he can see the whole picture, he will not be in a position to do so. Be sure, therefore, that you give him the whole story, all the facts. When an employee says, "But you didn't tell me that," you've done a poor join of delegating.

2. If necessary, take him around and introduce him to all the people who will be concerned with his new authority, and explain his job to them.

3. When you tell your employee about his additional job, be sure to tell him why you picked him. In other words, prepare him psychologically. Explain you confidence in him and his ability to do the job. Don't let him leave wondering, "Why did the boss pick on me to do another job when I already have more than I can do?" If he things you are pushing things off on him, he may embarrass you by doing a poor job.
4. Be sure you only delegate those things that you should. Don't push off the "hot potato" on an employee. Don't ask him to do an unpleasant job or one that you wouldn't do. And don't give him the job of discipline. That is a supervisor's job and should never be given to someone else.What's the Prime of Organization?

The purpose of organizing is to help up achieve goals. The first rule of organization, therefore, is to always remember what you are trying to do before you try to develop an organization to do it. Your goal, what you are trying to accomplish, should determine to a large degree what your organization looks like. A lot of people forget this and develop an organization that works but doesn't work well, because it was not developed with the job or goal in mind.

If your were called on to organize some men to build a reviewing stand for a parade, you wouldn't try to appoint a board of directors, a president, a sales manager, and so on, because that is not the kind of organization you need to get the stand built. Instead, you would probably hire yourself a couple of carpenters and tell them the size stand you want and where to get the materials. This is a temporary organization that will end as soon as the stand is built, and it does not have to be elaborate.

Contrast this hastily developed organization with one that would be needed to operate a bank. In a bank, you would want permanence, safety for depositors, compliance with state and federal banking laws, etc. In this instance, your objectives are different, and the organization structure will be different. You will need a board, a president, a controller, a loan officer—lots of people we didn't need for the organization to built the reviewing stand.

Even though you can easily see the different needs of these two organizations, a lot of papal overlook this rule when they begin to organize men. They often get carried away with the development of an organization and forget *why* the organization is being formed. Then they wind up with an eight-cylinder organization to do a two-cylinder job.

The rules, the, are:

1. First get clearly in mind what you want to accomplish.

2. Then build an organization to achieve what you want done.

Is unity of command important?

Unity of command means that every person in an organization has only one immediate superior who is his boss. In other words, only one person should give orders to an employee. Some companies are organized in such a way that sometimes two or more supervisors boss one man. This is poor organization for several reasons. If you have two or more bosses and you are conscientiously trying to do the work for all of them, you'll probably reach the point where you give up because of excess work, frustration, and maybe ulcers from worry.

Another reason that having two or more bosses is poor is that it provides a good place for a goldbrick to goof off. Neither boss knows what the employee is supposed to do, and he can loaf pretty much as he pleases. or it might end up as a situation where the "squeaking wheel gets the grease," that is, the boss who yells the loudest and beats the desk is the one who gets his work done. The other bosses take whatever time is left.

For all these reasons, having two or more bosses should be avoided. It helps nothing and resents all sorts of possibilities for conflicts.

What is the informal organization?

Every organization has two systems in operation: the *formal* and the *informal*.

The *formal* system is composed of the recognized and formalised lines of authority, communication, and control. This is the system we see "pictured" in the typical organization chart of a company.

The second or *informal* system is much more difficult to see and understand. In any group of employees, some leader always emerges. He sets the pace, and the others give him the authority to lead them. He is not the leader designated by management, but he has authority just as surely as the supervisor does. For example, in a sewing operation where a team of women work to produce certain parts of garments, one lay might emerge as the leader and spokesman for the group. Whatever she says should be done, the group does. If she tells the group to sew slower, they do it. If she says the thinks the group should complain to their supervisor about the quality of the material they are sewing, they will complain. Thus, she is the informal leader of a group who have organized themselves informally. This is not a formal organization structure set up by management. A supervisor can rescind or change a formal organization, but he cannot rescind or change an informal organization. The employees are the ones who set up the informal organization, and they are the ones who have the power to change it.

Some informal organizations are made up of employees who get together to get work done without the benefit of formal direction or authority. In a great many companies, these are the ones who actually make things go, who work with the sticky problems, and who give aid to the formal organization. However, they can also be just the opposite by being the ones who cause all the problems. It depends on their leadership and the direction their efforts take.

Every supervisor should recognize that informal organizations exist and that they are susceptible to human manipulation and opportunism because of their underfined structure. An informal organization might make trouble as well as give help. The alert supervisor, therefore, should try to develop a sensitivity to the presence of these informal organizations and be alert to possible problems they may cause before the problems faster and erupt as full-blown complaints or grievances.

Inasmuch as informal organizations are going to exist whether the supervisor likes them or not, a wise course of action might be to view them as a positive force, and use them to make the work of the department easier. This can be done by thinking of the informal leader not as a "ringleader", but as a person "in on things" whose talents can be used. By building good relations with him, the supervisor might get him to use his influence to settle a knotty problem between two employees or to give the supervisor help in getting some concept accepted by the workers.

What about the rumor mill?

News that comes from the rumor mill the grapevine, or the scuttlebutt is typically mere gossip that is unreliable, unconfirmed, and unauthenticated. Despite this lack of reliability, it draws people like a magnet,. and the rumors fly. We find it everywhere: in social circles, in small towns, in church, in schools, and in business. Not only is the information passed along by the rumor mull not reliable, it constantly changes in character as it is slanted to suit the purposes of the individual passing it one. For these and similar reasons, you should not take the "gospel" passed along by the grapevine as the "unmitigated truth." It just isn't. Instead, you should take all the information from the graphewine with the proverbial grain of salt. Don't let it disturb you. If it is true, it will be conformed later. The chances are, however, that it is pure rumor, which will be replaced hours later by an even better story. By all means don't take any action or make any decisions based on these rumors. Wait until you get the full story from management. You can help others by refusing to pass on information that you do not personally know to be true. A good rule is, Listen, but don't talk. Finally, if you must gripe and complain, do it to your supervisor or at home. Don't do it with a "trusted friend" at work. You may be providing him with more grist for the rumor mill.

What position should the supervisor take about the rumor mill? He should, of course, recognize that a graphevine exists in his department and should try to minimize the anxiety and worry it can cause his employees by feeding it with correct information instead of half truths. Although good information may not have the juicy intrigue that fabricated rumors have, it will give the rumormongers something to pass on and, being true, will give them the satisfaction of being "in the know." And, of course, the supervisor can do much to stem the flow of rumors by answering all questions as promptly and truthfully as he can. If employees know they can get the right information from their supervisor, this will do much to scotch the rumors.

Where does the supervisor fit into the organization?

The supervisor is the man who is frequently caught between the proverbial "rock and a hard place." He is the middle man who works with both labor and management. To the employees, he is "management." To the top managers, he is the low man on the managerial totem pole. He is, however, the key man in the organization structure.

On his shoulders rest the responsibility for correctly and tact-fully interpreting management's wishes to the workers. Because he works so closely with the employees, he is almost one of them and, in some cases, was one of them before his promotion. This may at times give him real problems with his loyalty. But because of this closeness, he is in the best position to correctly interpret the workers' feelings to top management. Being in this strategic position, the first-line supervisor is the key man in knitting both management and workers into a coordinated organization that works effectively and harmoniously to achieve its objectives.

Is it poor practice to communicate out of channels?

A channel is a normal path through which orders and communications flow from management to workers and vice versa. On an organization chart, the lines that join various jobs represent the usual channels of communication and chain of command. By chain of command, we mean the channel of communication from supervisor to supervisor through which orders flow from the top to the bottom man in the organization.

Most companies set u these channels carefully and for good reasons. They are the highways for orders and communications to follow, and as such, they keep everyone aware of what is going on. They serve to coordinate and unify the organization into a whole unit instead of a series of parts. When you leave these channels and take a shortcut, you are apt to run into problems. If an employee takes his grievance straight to the president of his company instead of his supervisor, he would be going out of channels. Most companies frown on going out of channels, so it is best to conform to the company's practices and wishes.

Sometimes, of course the normal channels of communication can delay work, and you might choose to take a shortcut and go around some individuals. If you do, be sure to tell those you bypassed, including your boss, what you have done and why. In this way, you will preserve the wholeness of the organization and keep your boss and others from thinking that your are doing things behind their backs.

Does span of management affect a supervisor?

You better believe it does! Span of management is

the number of people who report to a supervisor. If a supervisor has too many employees to look after, he will not be able to do a good job of supervising them. If he has too few, the company is not getting full value from him, and he may over-supervise and thereby destroy some of his employees' initiative. The problem is, how many employees can one supervisor effectively supervise? There is no magic answer, because the number that can be effectively supervised depends on a lot of things.

If all the people you supervise are in one room or area, you can supervise more employees than if they are scattered all over the plant. If all of them are doing the same thing, you can supervise more than if they are doing different things. With everybody doing the same job, you can tell them what to do in groups, thus saving time. Also, your work of planning, control, etc., will be easier, because everyone is doing the same job. If their work is interdependent, that is, if what one person does depends on what the next person does and so on, then you cannot supervise as many employees, because you will have to plan and watch the work closely to be sure that there is no bottleneck. If the people you supervise are very intelligent, you can supervise more than if the level of intelligence is very low. Most of the time, employees with a good education catch on quicker than those with a poor education. They don't, therefore, need as much supervision.

Another factor, of course, is the supervisor himself. Some people seem to have the ability to keep eight or ten irons in the fire, while others have difficulty looking after two or three. The supervisor who has the capacity to look after seven or eight things at once can supervise more employees than the supervisor who gets confused if he has over three or four items going.

Finally, factors like how exacting the quality standards are and how much time you have to get the work done have to be considered in trying to figure out the right number of employees for a supervisor to look after. As was stated earlier, there is no magic number. For one set to circumstances, the "right" number of employees for a supervisor to look after. As was stated earlier, there is no magic number. For one set of circumstances, the "right" number of employees for a supervisor might be 12. In another case, it might be 18 or 22 employees.

What has to be done is to consider the types of things that affect the span of management, look at the situation you have, and come up with a reasonable number. Experience will show if your judgement is wrong, and you can make adjustments.

Should a supervisor have an understudy?

Every supervisor needs someone he can call on to take over while he is out of the department. Even in the smallest departments, someone should be designed as an understudy or backup man. You never know when an emergency will call the supervisor away or when the opportunity will present itself for the supervisor to attend a conference or educational session. There are always vacation periods to be considered. And, of course, the supervisor himself may miss a promotion opportunity if no one has been groomed to take over. For these and other reasons that you can think of, every supervisor at one time or another will need a backstop. The problem is selecting the right man.

In choosing an employee to be your understudy, you should look for a person to whom other employees seem to turn naturally for help and advice about their work, a person who has the respect of the other employees, and a person who is regarded by them as a leader. He should be a level-headed individual who is able to handle problems without getting existed. He should be the type who wants to learn, has an open mind, and is motivated to accept larger responsibilities. And finally, he should have demonstrated his loyalty and dependability. You may not see all of these in a worker right away, but when given the opportunity to prove himself, you may find many latent or hidden qualities that weren't readily apparent.

Once you've decided on your understudy, it is not necessary to have a press conference to announce it. Instead you can start giving him small assignments to test his capacity and indicate your confidence in him. These will be signals to the other employees that it look like Sam Jones is learning your job. When you leave, of course, you should tell your department that Sam will be in charge until you get back.

There is no definite procedure that can be outlined for training every understudy. What will work in one case may not in another. You should, however, develop a plan to gradually bring Sam into focus on the details of how your department works, the reports issued, problem areas, and so on. If company policy allows it, you may also take Sam to supervisors' meetings so he can meet other supervisors and get a larger picture of the company's problems. Finally, you can give Sam the responsibility for certain areas or activities in your department to let him try his wings. Using steps similar to these, you should be able to gradually get Sam into a position to take over you department. And then, just when you think you've got him trained, you have to start the process all over because he is transferred out of you department to be the supervisor in another! But you've done an important managerial capacities. And you have given a fellow man an opportunity to try to improve himself.

What is the ideal organization?

Every supervisor should have in mind a plan for the perfect or ideal organization that he would like to have in his department. This would be the organization structure that in his mind would be most desirable and would best enable the department to achieve its objectives. The ideal organization might mean that old John, the strawboss, would not be in the picture. In might combine two or more jobs in a new operation. These things can't be achieved now because John has four more years before retirement, and you aren't going to change his job now. But having an ideal in mind is important, because when the time does come that a change can be made, you will have the change well in mind and can make it. When an employee suddenly leaves, it might present an opportunity for you to make a change *if you know what you want to do*. The ideal organization, then, provides the supervisor with a standard by which he can compare and evaluate his present organization, as well as give him a guide for making future changes when the opportunity presents itself.

What are the rewards of good organization?

An organization conceived and developed along the lines we have discussed will more than reward its leaders and members. No only will the firm and the employees' objectives be realized more easily and effectively with a good organization structure than with a poor organization, you will also find that the physical operation of the firm will be greatly enhanced. Things will go more smoothly. These ends are achieved because a good organization typically:

- Establishes responsibility and prevents "buck passing."
- Provides for easier communication.
- Eliminates jurisdictional disputes between individual.
- Helps develop executive ability.
- Aids in measuring a person's performance against his charges and responsibilities.

- Aids in equitable distribution of work functions and/or personnel supervision.
- Permits expansion and contraction without seriously disrupting the structure.
- In times of change, affords movement in the direction of the "ideal" organization.
- Makes for closer cooperation and higher morale.
- Points out "dead-end" jobs.
- Delineates avenues of promotion.
- Prevents duplication of work.
- Makes growth possible with adequate control and without literally killing top executives through overwork.
- Aids is wage and salary administration through forced job analysis and description.

8 Initiating Upward: The Supervisor Faces the Boss

Today's supervisor lives in a complex world. He must maintain good relations with his own subordinates. Between them there should be mutual feelings of trust and respect. He must perform his duties to the satisfaction of his immediate superior, who is his prime source of punishments and rewards. He must deal on occasion with direct pressures from levels further up the hierarchy—with the expectations and demands of his superior's boss or someone even higher. Then, too, he has frequent relations with other line and staff departments—some on the same status level, others *nominally* on the same level but actually in a position to give him orders—all of whose cooperation the supervisor needs to discharge his duties effectively.

These relationships would present fewer problems if the goals of the various individuals he depends on and the groups of which he is a member were the same. In the broadest sense, all management groups are committed to the goal of maximum profitability for the organization. But this over-reaching goal permits striking and frequently bitter divergences of opinion about how the goal can best be achieved, as well as endless power and status conflicts between managers. In these conflicts, the supervisor is frequently a witness or a victim.

Among the groups with which the supervisor is most intimately connected—the work group that he leads and the higher management group, that he immediately represents—there is not even an agreement on ultimate goals. True, few rank-and-file workers want to destroy the enterprise that employs them. They feel a stake in its survival to the extent that it fulfills their personal goals—good wages, a pleasant working atmosphere, the opportunity to do challenging, high quality work under conditions over which they exert some control, a guarantee of security for the future, and other satisfactions. Reasonable goals—all of them. But goals that, if fully realized, would clearly conflict with the overreaching corporate goal of maximum profit.

The man in the middle

More than twenty-five years ago, Fritz Roethlisberger of the Harvard Business School, in a classic article, described the foreman—the description would apply equally well to the first-line office or engineering supervisor—as "the man in the middle," endlessly subject to conflicting pressures and grievances from higher management and his own work group. Roethlisberger's description is valid for the supervisor. He is still the man in the middle.

The *effective* supervisor mediates successfully between his work group and management and discharges the obligations of his dual loyalty—to his subordinates and to his boss. The *ineffective* supervisor is caught in the crunch between the conflicting forces, sinks into inaction or succumbs to the pressure from one side or the other, and becomes useless to the organization.

The picture is the same as it was when Roethlisberger wrote about it in 1945, yet it is also altered. Wherein lie the changes? Actually, there are two differences: The controls, largely statistical, which higher management can use to check up on the performance of the supervisor and his work group are now more sophisticated, and the pressures the first-level supervisor can bring to bear on his subordinates are different and generally less effective.

How does the hierarchy limit the supervisor?

In most plants and offices with more than five hundred employees, higher management receives, in a weekly or daily basis, computer-processed data covering every quantifiable aspect of the supervisor's operation—pieces of paper processed by categories or components manufactured, lost time, absenteeism, scrap, rejects, tardiness, overtime, and every other production factor. Each item is meticulously flagged to call higher management's attention to any deviation from a predetermined standard of acceptability. True, twenty years ago higher management was receiving some of the same records. But it received them monthly or less frequently, if at all, and the records themselves were neither as comprehensive nor as accurate. The computer, with its ability to handle fantastic numbers of interrelated computations without man and without error, has tightened higher management's controls over its supervisors. Doomsday comes every Monday.

Affluence lessens the supervisor's power

The supervisor's position is further complicated and weakened by the decline in the economic pressures he can exert on his work group. Admittedly, these pressures have been exaggerated. The supervisor has always had to come to terms with the production-line workers, office girls, and engineers who do the actual work of the organization. They have always had the tacit power, the practicing malicious obedience, slowing down, wasting materials or spoiling work, and a hundred other subterfuges, to increase the supervisors costs and make him look had in the eyes of his superiors. To ensure output at a satisfactory level, the supervisor has made deals and guaranteed concessions to his work force, few of which would pass muster with higher management.

The difference is that in a period of comparatively full employment and affluence among workers, the supervisor's ultimate weapon—dismissal or the threat of it—has lost most of its past clout. Certainly, supervisors can and do fire employees. But we would guess that for each man fired today, five are retained only because the supervisor can't face the task of finding replacements for them. Threats, in other words, are out—way out—and persuasion is way in, as a means of maintaining production. But there's problem: The concessions many supervisors must make to keep the men working, we suspect, are greater and frequently more difficult to grant because of the sophisticated controls available to higher management.

Help is on the way

The picture has a compensating side. Higher management doesn't exist in a vacuum, and it is aware of the changes in the relative bargaining position of the supervisor vis a vis his work force. Roethlisberger commented that "the foreman was painfully tutored to focus his attention upward to his immediate superiors and the logic of evaluation they represented, rather than downward to his subordinates and the feelings they have." The statement, largely true in the 1950s, would not be true today. The supervisor has been taught and encouraged to empathize with his subordinates and even to feel loyalty toward them. Much of this new emphasis reflects the findings and teachings of behavioural scientists over the past two decades, but some also reveals a recognition usually unacknowledged, of the supervisor's weakened bargaining position.

We recall a conversation with a senior vice president of a large New England bank, a man who skillfully concealed any inner warmth he possessed. He described with considerable satisfaction the strategems employed by the bank to make its employees more productive, including paying 10 percent more in each job classification than its competitors. The goal of this effort: a 60 percent workday—that is, the bank's clerical force would do 60 percent as much work as the time-study people had determined they should be able to do without overexerting themselves. The vice president reported the success of the program and added complacently that other bank employees in the city were working a 50 percent day. The time-study engineers may have been mistaken—that's not important. The attitude of the banker is, and it's symbolic of the attitude among higher management generally. The big bosses don't expect the same level of production among rank-and-file employees as they did previously, and their diminished expectations have in turn lessened the pressure upon the supervisor.

The winning supervisory style

The implications seen plain. Said Machiavelli to his prince, "It is better to be feared than to be loved." But today's supervisor is hardly a sixteenth-century prince. He instead faces a situation in which it is very difficult for him to make his employees fear him. And he had better be loved if he is going to do a good job. In other words, the supervisor must master the arts of persuasion, and the ability to inspire the affection, or at least the respect, of his employees, if he wants to motivate them to a level of performance that will earn him the confidence and approval of higher management.

The winning supervisory style—one that would please bosses and subordinates alike—would appear to be a compromise. It would force subordinates to conform strictly to quantitative performance goals explicitly set and rigidly monitored by top management, but allow them maximum leeway in planning how to reach those goals and in most other aspects of plant or office behavior. For example, the quota for answering inquiries from correspondents is set at sixty a day, but the correspondent can decide whether she will plod along like the proverbial turtle and take a half-hour for lunch or will work at a breakneck clip and then spend two hours and a half out shopping.

The supervisor as imitator

Would that it were that simple. Several factors complicate the picture, of which the most important is that nine supervisors out of ten—we suspect the proper out of 100—imitate the style of supervision practiced by their immediate superior. If he is dictatorial and distrustful, always specifying each instruction to the last detail and forever checking to see whether his orders are being followed, so are the supervisors under him. If the superior is permissive and confident, allowing his supervisors to work within broad directives and interrupting only when something has gone wrong, so are they.

Close or general supervision?

Imitation the sincerest form of flattery? Maybe not. A question that leads into a semantic bog.

But among supervisors, imitation of their bosses is a form of flattery almost universally practiced. Those supervisors who are on the receiving end of *general* supervision are likely to practice it themselves. If they receive close supervision, they will supervise their subordinates closely.

Chris Arygris described, for example, a brilliant plant manager, the outstanding performer in a multiplant operation, who was constantly interceding, constantly checking, constantly controlling his supervisors. All of them respected him, all of them feared him, most them—perhaps surprisingly-liked him. And all of them did their best to act like him, including those who failed because his style went against the grain and they weren't good actors. Even the failures shared in the informal agreement that whoever first saw the plant manager in the morning would tell the rest what he's "hot on, today," and in turn they all would be "hot on" their own men and take the necessary steps to see that the manager would not "catch us with our plants down."

In exoneration, one point must be stressed. Even those supervisors whose natural style of supervision differed from the plant manager's were not guilty of unadulterated sycophancy. The plant manager was a rare composite of energy, intelligence, and devotion to work, obsessed with accomplishment and committed to rewarding it. With such a leader, supervisors will apparently forget their resentment over being closely controlled and even the general antagonism of the led toward the leader. They will complete fiercely for recognition and praise through the only medium the leader recognizes and rewards: excellence of performance.

Of course, imitation in an organization begins at the top. It's the total corporate climate that sets the style from which the supervisor's boss takes his cues, and which the supervisor, in turn, copies. However, it is not merely a process of above it. Managers are an initiative class, even what Walter Bagehot called the British middle class of a century ago, a "deferential" class.

The second factor is the one of controls. A top management that hoards all the decisions worth making unto itself—and surprisingly, this feat can be accomplished effectively in large organizations—obviously expects underlings at the various levels down the line to tread warily and interpret all policies and rules as literally as possible. Freedom exists only in the areas not covered by directives.

In a highly centralized organization, however, the supervisor is not likely to take advantage of even the limited opportunities for initiative. Instead, he will tend to play safe: When in doubt, don't. In an organization where many important decisions are delegated to levels below top management, the effect is similarly contagious. Managers at lower levels, including first-level supervisors, will show both flexibility in interpreting polices and initiative in handling matters covered by the rules. Whether or not they practice a general style of supervision will depend on the interaction between the requirements of the work situation and their own natural style. At least the option will be open to them.

Whether they *should* practice general supervision is a moot question. In any employee popularity poll, all the evidence indicates that it would win hands down. For example, a survey, conducted several years ago by Scott Meyers among more than thirteen hundred managers of all levels at Texas Instruments, shoed an overwhelming preference for a developmental manager over a reductive manager, regardless of the manager's values or style of supervision. The same survey also revealed that, of the managers rated as highly motivated, one-half had developmental bosses and only 8 percent had reductive bosses.

Yet we have seen that autocratic management and supervision can obtain outstanding results, at least in terms of production and what Emerson called "the unimpeachable judgment or an unbribable tribunal, the account of profit and loss." In a book written by Marrow, Bowers, and Seashore, a trio of experts prominently identified with the cause of participative management and general supervision, even they concede that the "'goodness' of any particular social organization and of any particular set of guiding principles for social progress lies not so much in its own inherent merit as in its utility for the effective use of work facilities and work process resources." In other words, the decision to employ general or close supervision should depend on the requirements of the particular work situation. Unfortunately, the decision is usually determined by the collective temperament of top management, which may match the requirements of the job, but frequently does not.

A little matter of influence

More important than the supervisor's style leadership in getting ahead with his bosses is his influence. Do other levels of management respond positively to his requests and recommendations? Does he have the skill to make effective presentations to his boss and to other managers within the organization? In short, can he sell himself and his ideas?

Incidentally, we feel that the supervisor who practices general supervision but has little or no influence with his superiors is almost certain to destroy his influence with his subordinates. For example, he calls a group meeting to discuss the problem of how to deal with excessive absenteeism. Then he takes his group's recommended solution to higher management, only to have it rejected out of hand. The experience is repeated several times with the same result. The group sinks into frustration and cynicism, becomes hostile and disrespectful to the supervisor. His position is barely tenable once his impotence has been exposed.

What gives a supervisor influence with his bosses? Performance is one part of the answer. Suppose a supervisor fails to measure up to the statistical indices used by top management to monitor and reward performance down the line. He is almost certain to be the subject of a confrontation between his boss and higher management—a confrontation from which his influence will emerge diminished or destroyed. Communication is also an important part of the answer. Success here lies not so much in the supervisor's manner of delivery or expertise in organizing the subject matter of his presentation as in the substance of his communications—what he tells the boss, and of almost equal importance, what he conceals from him. In subordinate-boss communications the substance is still the message.

Maintaining credibility

As a basic maxim of communication between subordinate and boss we commend: Tell him what he needs to know, not simply what he wants to hear, even when he has given unmistakable signs that he doesn't want to hear all the facts. We know of a case where the machinery on a conveyer line had become too light for the production load, causing frequent breakdowns and the replacement of bearings, drive belts, sprockets, and other parts. The supervisor knew a major installation was in order, but each time he approached the plant superintendent he got the Typhoid Mary treatment, and eventually he subsided. Production was being maintained at the expense of excessive overtime when the day of reckoning arrived. The plant manager called for an accounting and the supervisor was on the spot. Should he take the blame, or should he be disloyal to the superintendent, his immediate superior? He "took the count" and hoped that his superior would repay his loyalty. Who can say that he decided wrong? He owned his job to his boss. And besides, he had to balance the temporary gratitude and protection of the plant manager against the possibility of permanent hostility and continuing retaliation from his immediate superior.

We weren't surprised to hear the results of a study made to determine why some boss-subordinates communicated and others did not. The finding of the study? The most accurate and extensive communication took place between a boss and a trusting subordinate who didn't care about getting ahead.

Empathy works

Most bosses want the truth and appreciate it, at least in the long run—the previous case notwithstanding. In another situation with which we are familiar, the superintendent steadily resisted pressures from quality control for a lower scrap-and-reject rate on two grounds, one explicit, the other hidden. He didn't want to add the expense of hiring more inspectors to his budget, and he feared that higher-quality work would mean lower production—and production was the *idee fixe* of his boss, the plant manager. The easy position for the supervisor was to sympathize and agree with his boss. "If we went along with those goddam perfectionists in quality control, nothing would even get out the door." However, the supervisor said nothing of the kind. He empathized with his boss instead of sympathizing with him, and recognizing that more inspectors would contribute to the company's—and the superintendent's—good, he took a stand in favor of adding them. In time, his pressure was influential in persuading the superintendent to modify his position. The superintendent probably never thought fondly of the supervisor for standing up to him. But he respected his integrity and recognized his credibility. People—and bosses are people too—have a deep and well-founded respect for someone who sticks to what he believes is the truth and who shows he is interested in nothing less.

Empathy can boomerang

Not all bosses can tolerate openness. Sometimes the truth hurts too much to accept. Take the case of the direct-mail supervisor for a magazine-publishing company that sold some of its periodicals by means of premium booklets on subjects assumed to be of interest to potential subscribers. The publisher of one magazine was a man who preached quality to his subordinates, but who at the same time impressed his bosses by repeatedly demonstrating how costs could be cut at the expense of quality—with little or no loss of sales.

The most recent premiums, written by hacks at bargain-basement prices, had been judged unusable by the publisher. The direct-mail chief saw his opportunity and seized it. He wrote a memo to the publisher in which he stated the case for higher-quality premiums in the strongest terms of which he was capable. Among his statements were these:

Evidence suggests we are not competitive. We should commission premiums from people who know their subjects thoroughly, but at our rates the experts won't write for us.

Premiums obtained at our price have been money thrown away. I can't resist quoting Ruskin's warning. "But when you pay too little, you sometimes lose all, because the thing you bought was incapable of doing the thing it was bought to do!"

The publisher never answered the memo or even alluded to it in any future contacts with the supervisor. His answer who had tactfully submitted a much milder document on the same general topic—the need to improve quality. Apparently the publisher didn't trust his own self-control enough to risk a direct confrontation with the first supervisor, who had challenged his self-image so painfully. At any rate, the direct-mail supervisor's days of influence with the boss ended abruptly with the delivery of his memo.

Through a frequent and painful paradox, the supervisor is required to limit his communications to his boss in order to maintain his influence with him. There are things the boss would like to know, that he may need to know, that policies and regulations require that he know. But sometimes these things must be withheld from him so that the performance level in the supervisor's operation can be maintained at a satisfactory level.

Obligated to make a choice, the supervisor has to balance his fears. If he conceals the facts, the boss may discover the deception and penalize him—a real but indeterminate fear, since both the risks and the penalties are difficult to calculate. If he tells the truth, the price of his honesty will be the impaired performance of his work group, the almost certain loss of influence with the boss, and penalties once the performance drop becomes obvious. Faced with this dilemma, most supervisors opt for deception.

Take the supervisors described by Dalton. They were under intense pressure from higher management to increase production and driven into various departures from official procedure in order to retain influence with their bosses and win their approval.

The pay rate varied with the product specifications, and several supervisors through an informal deal with their work groups, rearranged the order sequence to permit the higher-paying orders to be run first, regardless of the scheduling. The deal, of course, was in direct violation of company regulations and threw the supervisors into conflict with production planning, which had worked out a rigid sequence for processing orders based on delivery deadlines promised to customers.

We would assume that the supervisors couldn't get away with an evasion so bald-faced. Not so. Production planning threatened the supervisors involved, who first played dumb and then contrived elaborate excuses to conceal their departures from schedule. What happened when production planning confronted higher plant management with evidence of what the supervisors were up to? Very little Higher management condemned the supervisors' actions for the record but enforced no penalties, and the practice continued. Of course the supervisors' deal was contrary to the rules, but one fact overshadowed any other consideration: Total production in the departments that had broken the rules was much higher than it had been before.

Perhaps the supervisors had anticipated the tacit approval of higher management when they circumvented the rules, although we doubt it. Instead, when faced with the pressure for higher production, they made a deal with their workers that ensured it, then crossed their fingers and prepared to take the consequences if and when their arrangements were disclosed to higher management.

The indispensables

Not every case of deception involves the supervisor's concealing facts from his boss because of pressure from his subordinates. Sometimes it's the supervisors themselves who take advantage of their strategic position and apply pressure on their bosses to circumvent the rules. We're familiar with one case involving two copy supervisors in the Cleveland office of a New York advertising agency. The agency is notorious for the strictness and minuteness of its regulations, and the resident vice president is equally notorious for his zeal in enforcing them. One motto of the organization is that "there is no such thing as being a little bit late." Obviously, one of the V.P.'s responsibilities was to uphold the no-tardiness rule and discipline violators.

The two supervisors systematically began to violate the rule, coming in first a few minutes late each morning, then gradually extending their tardiness to a half-hour or forty-five minutes. The V.P. closed his eyes to the practice but after several weeks he took reluctant cognizance. The senior of the two laid it on the line—he would resign rather than obey the rule—and the V.P. promptly caved in.

That's not the end of the story. The two supervisors continued to do good work, thus keeping their end of the silent bargain, but the extent of their tardiness reduced the rule to a travesty. Being an hour late became standard operating procedure. Other supervisors and employees imitated the two copy chiefs, feeling that the V.P. would not crack down on them either, and they were correct. There was one curious side effect. Out of fear, guilt, or a combination of both, the V.P. became more unrelenting than ever in rigidly enforcing every last petty regulation in the shop, apparently seeking to compensate by his zeal in other areas for his backsliding with tardiness.

Bypassing the boss

Another practice calculated to endanger relations with the boss, but one that supervisors sometimes feel justified in, or even driven to, adopting is bypassing the boss. Sometimes quick action is imperative and there just isn't time to contact the boss, or he's out of town or otherwise not available.

One supervisor described his strategy this way: "I am always in a position of getting people to waive the formal requirements. Recently a manager said he couldn't do it without the authorization of may boss. I told him I could sign for my boss. I just had a get that approval that day. Of course, as soon as I could I went to my boss to make sure he was in agreement with my action."

Another innocent and necessary form of bypassing the boss is cutting the red tape involved in going through channels. For example, in a small manufacturing company the accounting department was located directly across the hall from research and development. Everyone recognized that scientists and engineers kept odd hours and everyone accepted this practice. What the clerks in accounting wouldn't accept and repeatedly griped about to their boss was that the clerks in R and D felt that they too were privileged characters with no obligation to keep regular hours.

What could be accounting supervisor do about the problem? If he followed the rule book, he would report the matter to his supervisor. It would travel on up the line to the common superior of both accounting and R and D, and then down the line again till it reached the presumptuous clericals in R and D.

In this situation we suspect nine supervisors out of ten would cross the hall for a face-to-face talk with their opposite number and try to resolve the problem on the spot. Going through channels would be the last resort. It always takes time and frequently complicates the problem. Think of what would happen in a hospital if, say, an oxygen tank goes out of order. If everybody always followed channels, the nurse would report to the head nurse, she to the chief engineer, and he to the repairman. The patient would probably be dead before the equipment was fixed.

Of course, the supervisor who cuts red tape always runs the risk that what's decided upon at his level will be over-ruled by his superior at one level of the hierarchy or another, sometimes on the merits of the case and sometimes out of someone's pique at being "short-circuited." However, it's a risk most supervisors feel is worth taking.

Revenue bypassing

A variation of bypassing, and obviously one over which the supervisor has no control, is played by the big boss himself when he bypass one or more levels of management to find out directly from the supervisor what is happening—for example, in the production shop or the filed sales force. Top management is frequently dissatisfied with the quality of reports that filter up to it and wonders what is really going on, especially when it seems to be going on badly. We are reminded of Haroun-al-Raschid of *Arabian Nights* fame who, so the legend goes, would emerge from his palace at night dressed as an itinerant traveler, and mingle with his subjects to discover what they really thought about him and his regime. The same story told about kings and other potentates symbolizes an important fact: Status, power, and sheer size tend to isolate the top man from the truth.

In large organizations where the top men view operations mostly through the eyes of others, experience often leads them to distrust the evidence of those eyes. So they decide quite literally to see for themselves. Here is a description of a former president of Curtis Wright, who was famous—some say, notorious—for being his own chief troubleshooter.

Effects on the supervisors

What's wrong with bosses like Hurley who cut red tape and get down to the grass roots by a direct approach to supervisors or even their subordinates? Given the way Hurley and others like him handle their bypassing of the channels of authority, a great deal. They give the responsible executive no time to take corrective action before they rush in and take over. They diffuse their energies and ultimately their authority too thin instead of saving these assets for the problems where it is appropriate to lay them on the line.

The top manager who dashes in, unbriefed and unexpected, to take charge inevitably damages the organization from the standpoint of the supervisor. If the superior has the right answer or selects the man who can come up with it, the supervisor concludes quite logically that the big boss views everyone between himself and the supervisor and the supervisor as incompetent and to be ignored. If the big boss makes a mess out of the situation, if he doesn't have the answer or dumps the solution into the hands of the wrong man, his incompetence will undermine the supervisor's confidence in the whole organization. The subordinate has seen the clay feet and the image will never look the same again.

Bypassing can be a virtue, even a necessity. General Horrocks of the British Army, for example described the circumstances under which bypassing is desirable, and his specifications can easily be translated from the military to a business organization when the pressure is on in an emergency

The supervisor acts on his own

Not at all innocent and extremely risky is the tactic used by the supervisor who makes decisions on his own, overruling the boss or ignoring him because he believes that his superior has decided wrong or would do so if he had the chance. A classic case involves the origin of the phrase "turning a blind eye." Lord Nelson ignored the instruction issued by his superior to break off his engagement at the battle of Copenhagen, clapped the telescope over his blind eye—and own the battle. The problem of playing this game is that it is almost as dangerous to win as to lose. There's no possible defense in case of failure, and the best that the supervisor can hope for if he makes the right decision is forgiveness from his boss-and grudging forgiveness at that.

What's the worst? Take the case of a general superintendent who was asked by his boss, the plant manager, to represent him at the monthly budget review. The plant manager warned him against accepting a recommendation for a lot of costly new equipment from Vince Reilly, superintendent of building Two, but added, "Don't get into an argument with Reilly if you can help it." The meeting came and Reilly made his recommendation, but here the general superintendent departed from the script. Reilly's arguments impressed him and the others at the meeting so much that the suggested, and the group approved, a decision to purchase a single item of the new equipment to help determine whether a major investment would be justified. A week later, when the plant manager was back on the job, he vetoed the purchase and fired the general superintendent, making the undeniable point, "I spelled out exactly what I wanted you to do. If I had wanted you to do my thinking for me, I would have told you so." Our sources tell us that Reilly was right and that the compromise initiated by the general superintendent was an intelligent decision, if he had been free to ignore the human element—his boss's prejudices and instructions. He wasn't—he did—and he paid the price.

Over the boss's head

Now let's consider the royal flush in bypasses: going over the boss's head and appealing to his superior or even some one higher up. Nothing could be more dangerous for a subordinate. His job invariably will be at stake. But under two circumstances, a supervisor may decided to proceed. When he feels his supervisor is incompetent and he has to secure recognition from some one else or quit, and when he believes so passionately in an idea or project which his boss opposes that he is willing to lay his job on the line for the chance to win his point.

Does it work?

An example of the first occurred several years ago in the advertising department of a large furniture company. A young copywriter, ambitious, intelligent and convinced of his worth, found that his most original ideas and crispest copy invariably landed in the boss's wastebasket. He had decided to resign, but before leaving he tried a desperate strategem. After all, what did he have to lose? He assembled several of the advertisements the company had run together with his own version of each ad, sent the package to the company president, and awaited the results. He did not have long to wait. Within a week he was transferred to another supervisor, and within a month his old boss had left the company. Furthermore, he was never far from the president's eye after that. Today, he's a senior vice president and advertising is merely one of the functional areas for which he is responsible.

Another man who risked all and won was a young naval lieutenant at the turn of the century, William S.Sims. He was convinced that continuous-aim firing, introduced into the British Navy in 1898, had revolutionized naval gunnery and changed it from an art to a science. Obviously, the American Navy had to follow suit. In thirteen official reports to the Bureau of Ordnance and the Bureau of Navigation, Sims documented the case for continuous-aim firing, supporting his arguments with masses of factual data. The reactions of the naval brass? Dead silence, followed by derision of his claims and finally, name-calling in desperation, Sims wrote to the commander in chief, Theodore Roosevelt, and presented him with the evidence. The President's reaction was swift. He installed continuous-aim firing in the US Navy, and made Sims inspector of target practice, a position he held for the last six years of Roosevelt's administration. Sim's personal mark had been made. He rose rapidly, and capped a distinguished career by serving a s chief of naval operations in World War I.

The boss is still there

We have cited two instances where going over the boss's head paid off spectacularly, and where the game was worth the candle. These are the exceptions. In 99 cases out of 100, the supervisor who makes an end run around his boss or when important plans are being formulated or results analysed. Bypassing gives the man at the top a chance to evaluate the quality of younger managers, to get authentic information, and to obtain proposals and appraisals firsthand from the men who generated them. And another specification of Horrocks which is just as important in business: Always invite the man's immediate superior; to be present at any discussion.

What the top man loses in frankness and openness of communication is compensated for by what he gains in retaining the confidence and the position of the superior. When a confidential session between a supervisor and his boss's superior is really called for, it is time to consider whether one of them should not leave the organization or at least the organizational unit. If they're both valuable men, their relationship has deteriorated to the point where one man's potential is going to be better realized somewhere else-within the organization or outside it.

The open door

Finally, of course, the supervisor can himself be the victim of a bypass. Many companies maintain an open-door policy. The rank-and-file employee has the privilege of walking into the office of any manager in the organization, upto and including the president, and voicing his complaint or making his suggestions. In most cases, however, the open-door policy is a fiction. The door may be open but somehow the rank-and-file employee seldom crosses the threshold.

The reasons aren't hard to fathom. The social distance between the average hourly employee and typical higher management is too great. More important, just as the supervisor hesitates to bypass his boss because he is the prime source of all penalties and rewards, the rank-and-file employee hesitates before he bypasses the supervisor. He balances, usually unconsciously, the slim chance of winning anything from his appeal against the danger of losing a great deal.

Another limitation of the open-door policy, even in organizations that sincerely subscribe to it, is the natural reluctance of higher managers to make it too effective. They are interested in creating a viable appeal channel, but they are not interested in spending great quantities of time listening to petty grievances and trivial or worthless suggestions from every clerk or assembly-line worker.

Take the case of the man in the welding shop who read in a trade magazine about some new equipment. In his role as a stockholder in the company-he owned twenty shares-he wrote the president, recommending the purchase of the equipment, In return, the welder got a warm letter from the president, commending his interest, promising to investigate his recommendation, and concluding with an invitation to communicate with him whenever , there was something he felt the president should be aware of. The presidents' polite gesture-at least we take it as that-triggered an avalanche of suggestions. The welder swaggered around the shop boasting about his buddy Frank in Chicago. Finally, one night while under the influence, he called Frank to describe in vivid terms what he thought of his immediate boss. The next morning saw the finale-an ultimatum from the plant manager:

That the case is extreme, we agree, But it illustrates an important and difficult problem for higher management: on the one hand, how to encourage the rank-and-file employee to bypass his supervisor when his complaint or suggestion is legitimate and significant, and on the other, how to discourage him from using the open door when the complaint or suggestion is small and has little merit.

What is the supervisor's attitude toward the open-door policy? Doesn't it worry him when his disgruntled employees go to higher management with troublemaking problems, false charges, or tales out of school? Obviously, although he's probably even more concerned when the tales are not only unfavourable but also true.

How the supervisor feels toward the open-door policy depends heavily on two factors: the degree to which he has removed himself from his own men, and the approach the big bosses takes with his subordinates. Many times a subordinate bypasses the supervisor because he feels, "What's the use?". The supervisor has made it plain in the past that he has neither the time nor interest to listen to his subordinates' complaints or ideas. The supervisor who hasn't heard from his men recently about any problems may be the rare but lucky man whose department has no problems. More likely, he's the supervisor who has gotten the message across that he doesn't want to hear that anything is wrong in his department. He has only himself to blame if his men choose to forget that he is one of the channels through which they should go.

Making the open door work

What does the boss do when he's approached by an employee with a gripe against his supervisor? Steer a delicate course between Scylla and Charybdis-between encouraging bypassing and sabotaging the supervisor's morale on one hand, and banning the bypassing thereby having a disastrous effect on the workers' morale, on the other. If the subordinate has not already talked to the supervisor, the boss's preferred course of action is plain: He should listen sympathetically but noncommittally, then refer the subordinate back to his supervisor. What if the subordinate has talked to the supervisor and his failure to obtain any satisfaction from him is precisely what has landed him on the boss's doorstep? What does the boss say then? Up to a point, he follows the same script, listening sympathetically but noncommittally, even if it appears obvious that the supervisor is at fault. At the end of the talk, he confines himself to a promise that he will talk to the supervisor and that the supervisor will, in turn, be in touch with the employee.

From there on, it is more difficult to prescribe the course of action. Too much depends on the men involved and the circumstances. An autocratic boss confronted by a pigheaded and stupid supervisor, might find it a necessity as well as a pleasure to administer a brutal tongue-lashing. Nothing less would take. However, even under those circumstances, the boss should take great care to see that the rank-and-file employee knows nothing about how he handled the problem. It should be the supervisor who explains the change of position to the subordinate, not the boss, and wherever possible, the decision should be presented as a case of the supervisor's having changed his mind, not of having had his mind changed for him. Obviously the employee, knowing the stubbornness of his boss and his past opposition, will suspect the true story. But the continuing authority and prestige of the supervisor requires the big boss to maintain the myth that the supervisor made the final decision. Otherwise, his every decision could be challenged by anyone who disagreed with it and his position would become untenable.

Speaking up for his men

One final problem area in upward communications casts the supervisor in a position where frank speaking may get him into immediate difficulty with his superiors, and silence will get him into trouble with his subordinates and may ultimately undermine his effectiveness in helping management gain its objectives. We're talking about the supervisor's responsibility to protect his subordinates' interests and represent them to higher management. His is the duty to speak out on their behalf when higher management has made what he and they feel is a wrong decision.

Some supervisors fulfill this role admirably. Consider, for example, what one worker said about his foreman. "My present foreman is the nicest guy I have ever worked for. The other foremen respect him also. I saw him stick his neck out with the general foreman over work loads. He will argue a point with the general foreman if he thinks he is right."

However, there is considerable evidence to suggest that this foreman is in the minority. One study conducted by the Opinion Research Corporation showed that only 12 percent of the hourly workers interviewed rated their supervisors as "good" in handling questions and complaints, and another study showed that nearly half the employees agreed with the statement that an employee who told his immediate supervisor everything he felt about the company would probably get into a lot of trouble. "Many employees believe," concluded Alfred Vogel, research director of the Opinion Research Corporation, "that their bosses are paid to block criticism from going up the line." Incidentally, supervisors had a very different perspective on themselves. In dealing with their employees' problems, most asserted that they "almost always" or "usually" take prompt action.

The dilemma of dual loyalty

What's the reason for the generally poor performance of supervisors in representing the interests of their subordinates to higher management? The easy answer is fear to retaliation from higher managers, the paradox being that the more credit a man gets from below, the less he gets from above. Credit from below comes when a supervisor questions every unwelcome decision from above and protests vigorously and repeatedly any time higher management has done wrong by one of his subordinates. The dilemma is real enough, but let's not exaggerate its importance. The supervisor, as we have seen, has dual loyalties-to both management and subordinates- but only the most Neanderthal of managements fail to recognize the existence of this duality or attempt to monopolize his allegiance. The more sophisticated managements know that his duality works to their advantage even when, or perhaps most when, the supervisor's loyalties are weighted in the direction of his employees. A study conducted by the Prudential Life Insurance Company indicated that out or eleven high production supervisors, nine identified themselves more with their employees than with the company. Among low producing supervisors, the reverse was true: Eight of them identified themselves with the company and only two with their employees. The same pattern was repeated in the attitude toward separate dining rooms for supervisors. The high-production supervisors reflected the attitude of their employees and objected to the segregation, while the low-production supervisors went along with it. The wage contract apparently buys the minimum level of performance—conscience and fear motivate employees only up to a point.

Performance beyond this point is the result of many factors, not the least of which is loyalty of the employees to the supervisor and their desire to make him look good. Obviously, he must earn this loyalty, and his most effective way of doing so is by representing their interests to higher management.

Recognition of dual loyalty

As we have pointed out, most higher managements are aware of, and even encourage the supervisors' dual loyalty. But in some companies they don't recognize it: They rebuff the supervisors' every attempt to represent their employees' interests, frequently adding gall and wormwood by complaining that the supervisor isn't acting like "a company man." Here, we can end our search for the reasons why the supervisor isn't doing a better job of speaking out for his subordinates. He isn't allowed to, and if he persists, he probably will lose his job.

The umbrella of top management's demands, however, isn't broad enough to cover all circumstances where supervisors renege on their responsibilities of representing their subordinates. Some rather ugly factors also enter into the picture—to be specific, arrogance and a sense of social distance. Most supervisors have a low opinion of the capabilities of the employees who work for them. A survey of five hundred managers showed that the managers in every group rated their subordinates and rank-and-file employees well below themselves, particularly on responsibility, judgment, and initiative. When the supervisor fails to speak up for an employee, he is showing him how little he thinks of him. At the same time, he is reasserting and reinforcing his own sense of superiority. After all, if the employee's judgment were equal to the supervisor's, the issue would never have been raised.

And the supervisor is doing something else: By showing that he is 100 percent "a company man." he emphasizes his social distance from his employees. We usually think of social distance in terms more innocent or harmless - the supervisor up from the ranks stops bowling with the boys on Fridays, drifts out of the social club where some of his men spend their spare time; or quits having a round of boilermakers at the shift's end. None of these are as dramatic as failing to speak up-this clearly emphasizes the message: "I've left the boys behind. I'm 'a company man' now."

Why should some supervisors be so compulsive on this score? Chester Barnard, in his classic study, Functions of the Executive, captured the pathology of their behavior when he wrote, "The nearer one in authority over workers himself stands to the workers in respect of origin, education, occupational capacity, and level of earnings, the more violently self-assertive will be the manifestations of his will-to-power, the more insistent he will be in a display of authority, and more sharply will he therefore come into conflict with the worker's sense of self-esteem."

What Barnard wrote we think applies only to

a virulent minority, but with that minority, we subscribe to the indictment. Human nature wears many masks to hide from itself. Some supervisors who fail to represent their subordinates rationalize their failure as due to fear of retaliation from higher management when the real reasons are located deep and unacknowledged in their own nature.

Of course, as we noted before in talking about supervisory styles, the particular style of the supervisor has less effect upon his employees than whether this style has helped him win influence with his bosses and peers. His skill in this area is revealed when he speaks up for his men. Employees respect the boss who represents their interests, but if the representations almost always fail because the supervisor's low level of performance, ineptness in handling his other upward communications roles, or both have destroyed his influence with higher management, his repeated failures will in the end forfeit his employees' esteem. It is not enough for the supervisor to be a man of good will. Influence fosters respect; impotence destroy it.

What is good supervisory performance?

We postulated that the superiors' influence with higher management depends largely on two factors: his personal skill in upward communications and his level of performance as recorded by a complex network of statistical controls. We have seen the delicate, even torturous course he faces in his communications with higher management. By comparison, his job of impressing his bosses with his superior performance should be straightforward.

To determine whether or not the supervisor is doing a good job, all higher management needs to do is look at the figures covering key factors such as production levels, percentage of scrap and rejects, man-hours expended per unit of production, tardiness, and turnover. It's all down in black and white - and figures never lie.

The unmeasurables

Figures never lie, but sometimes they omit - and omissions frequently conceal the true facts of performance. Any attempt to measure performance through statistics fails to get at the whole truth because some elements of the supervisor's performance are very difficult to measure, and others, such as the supervisor's success in maintaining the morale of his department, resist statistical measurement. These inherent weaknesses of statistical controls have two consequences, both of them unfortunate for the supervisor and higher management. His superiors get a picture of the supervisor's performance that is distorted and that doesn't reflect his real value to the organization. The supervisor, in an effort to impress higher management, concentrates on those areas of his operation where success can be quantified and where it is certain to be recognized—and, he hopes, rewarded.

In most industrial operations, cost accounting has developed "standard costs" for every item produced. If the standard cost of an item is 45 cents and the supervisor's department can make it for 43 cents, he is a hero. But if he makes the same item for 49 cents, he is a bum. Sounds fair enough, and it would be, except for two things. First, cost accounting is far from an exact science - figures may never lie, but they're only as accurate as the input from the frequently fallible and occasionally devious industrial engineers who set the standards in the first place. Second, standards may be too"light" or too "loose" because of an error, or occasionally they may be too "tight" because the industrial engineer feels it's his job to build pressures for top performance into the standard. In these instances, the supervisor is either penalized or rewarded by the defective standard, and higher management gets a false picture of his performance.

Then we have the areas, such as morale, that most supervisors tend to neglect - and for good reason. Because such areas are so hard to measure, higher management has no yardstick with which to judge the supervisor's performance. So it usually overlooks them completely when the time comes to hand out pay and perquisites. Good employee relations are something a supervisor may get around to worrying about when he's sure his costs are in line, his production is up to snuff, and his scrap rate is well within the allowable limits. Developing his men is a similar area. The personnel department exhorts supervisors to develop their men for positions of greater responsibility and usefulness, but we have never heard of a supervisor's receiving a bonus or any other form of explicit recognition for his developmental prowess. Until we do, we expect that supervisors will continue to gold brick on their developmental function.

Measurement: the enemy of performance

When statistical data are the prime means of evaluating success or failure, supervisors will sometimes go a long way to show up well on paper. Figures never lie but they can be "adjusted." In one department, men tossed defective parts into trash cans, with their supervisor's full knowledge and tacit approval. The reject count, naturally, was below average. In another department, the supervisor himself came back at night to collect the rejects and dump them into a local quarry. In the morning, there would be nothing to count in the trash cans.

And figures are juggled. An engineering supervisor in an electronics company, whom we know, recently submitted a quarterly budget that allotted many man-hours to a project that was nearly finished, and assigned only a few hours to a project, already way over its budget, that needed many more hours to complete. The supervisor's reasoning was obvious: The juggling wouldn't cost the company any more money, and unless higher management found out the truth, it would get him off the hook.

Index